M000035127

OPEN LATE

New and Collected Poems 1979–2018

REX WILDER

BOOKS BY REX WILDER

POETRY

Waking Bodies (2006)

Beauty and the Books, with photographs by Vanessa Rudloff (2008)

Boomerangs in the Living Room (2013)

OPEN LATE

NEW AND COLLECTED POEMS 1979–2018

REX WILDER

EDITED BY

Phil Bevis and Jamaica Baldwin

CHATWIN BOOKS

SEATTLE, 2018

Poems copyright 1979–2018 Rex Wilder.
Editorial and design copyright Chatwin Books 2018.
All rights reserved.

Series design by Katrina Noble. Interior typesetting by Cyra Jane Hobson,
cover typography by Annie Brulé. The author and publisher thank Megan Gray
and Jessica Hornik for their editorial assistance.

Volume II in the *Chatwin Collected Poets* series.

hardcover signed limited edition ISBN 978-1-63398-066-2
hardcover ISBN 978-1-63398-069-3
paperback ISBN 978-1-63398-067-9

Visit us online at www.ChatwinBooks.com.

DEDICATION

love for

Jess, beyond words

my Briskin parents, Judy and Bernie

my Wilder parents, Annie and Jack

Madeline, Simon, and Oliver

TABLE OF CONTENTS

PREFACE

Welcome to the collected poetry of Rex Wilder, whose passion for rhyme and rhymes of passion have long set him apart as a unique presence in contemporary American poetry. With a handful of notable exceptions, traditional rhyming poetry has been seen as antiquated, stuffy, and constrictive since the middle of the last century. Wilder is one of the few poets of stature to consistently employ it and, more than that, to reinvigorate it. To celebrate it. Rhyming poets from prior generations, like Frost, have remained popular with readers, but in the contemporary canon and major poetic schools, rhyme has been something of an orphan.

Open Late contains Wilder's previously published work, dating back to his first published poem in 1979. The collection also includes some hundred works never before in print. In addition to this new work, the author has revised many of his earlier poems. The collection thus represents not just a compilation of what *has been,* but the author's affirmation of what his body of work *should be.*

Much of Wilder's work is about love, in all its facets, from that joy of first discovery, through passion, the warmth of shared dailiness, heartbreak, and a sometimes shattering aftermath. Many of his real romances are memorialized here faithfully, while others serve as a jumping-off point for his invention, a bucket dropped into a wishing well. In an extended series of poems featuring the fictitious character of Séverine, Wilder drinks her in and is sustained by her. The poet courts her, drawing her into our imaginations, until we, too, can feel this woman, what she sees and whom she loves, over a lifetime of days.

Wilder writes himself out of the abyss through the mythical Séverine, who represents all women and none. She lives and breathes, but never existed—or so Wilder wants us to believe. She is his hope and longing, his joy and ennui. She is his past, present, and future. We see Wilder's love for rhyme here representing his faith in love and romance. He takes the joy of one and gives to another—searching for the ideal song, the ideal other. There is a rhyme for everything, of this the poet is certain—a response for every call.

The subject of fatherhood and children is the other emotional linchpin of Wilder's work. In these poems, his wonderment at unexpected joy comes alive on the page. Elsewhere, he shows us aspects of work, travel, and life that we never expected or thought to notice. But it is his idolatry of love and family that makes Wilder's poetic voice unmistakably his own.

Beyond his decades-long effort carrying the torch of rhyme, Wilder's unique contribution to the craft of poetry is the invention of the boomerang, which the late Richard Wilbur, one of the greatest American poets, once called with a wink "admirable throwaways." Boomerangs are four-line haiku-like works that rhyme the first word or syllable with the last. As Wilbur said, "a thrown boomerang has three phases: it flies to first base (as it were), then travels over to third and rises, then swoops home." The form of Wilder's boomerang captures this trajectory.

The two-term U.S. poet laureate Billy Collins said of Wilder's first book, *Waking Bodies*, whose poems are included in this volume:

> In Rex Wilder's poetry, the tired English of everyday use comes back to us refreshed and full of its original surprise. In a world glutted with poetry, that Wilder has found a new way to say the old things is a notable achievement.

An outlier in this sense in the world of contemporary poetry, Wilder has recently found that his fascination with rhyme was right at home in the scenes of hip hop and other musical genres. In fact, in the past several years he has been actively collaborating with songwriters. His work as a lyricist has immersed him more deeply in the power of rhyme, and has sparked new energy for his poetic work.

So often a volume of collected poems signifies a culmination, an ending. But the preparation of this volume has been marked by one of the most productive periods in the author's career, an explosion of new work and creative energy. It would seem to presage not an ending, but a renewal, a new beginning—something a little like love.

The Editors

Love in All Its Facets

REX WILDER

I

CHASE AND THE PASSION

Summers on Woodland

Relaxation we'd later know
sexually: premonition of afterglow
in swimming holes, in sunlight
cut by Rousseau's forest. Coat
after sheer coat of water tried
on and rejected by the heat.
We were ten forever, tethering
our parents' ages too; weathering
the summer thunderstorms
of childhood, staying out of harm's
way as we dripped and dried
off under lemon trees, a pride
of cubs, printed with grape leaves'
shadows and the rest of our lives.

Dôme du Goûter

I need your help to bring this poem to an end.
I stopped short of God yesterday, or the light that lies
behind the bend of the mind.
A mirror was called for: I doubled for you.
I witnessed the unflawed instant, an inch of skyless air
wild and crying, caught between the palm of a cloud
and the ceiling of a domed glacier.
Take this poem into a room without your phone or a lover
and close your eyes between the lines. The light
is the blue that defines a pine tree or a shoulder blade
in the mountains at dusk, between specter-blue
and blue erasure, an emptiness into which you pour yourself
like fountains into sun. Be alone in the moment endowed
to me briefly, where the sky is scored
with the paths of birds just passed, already-thought
thoughts waiting for words.

Outpost

Allow me all or nothing,
allow me to surpass love,
allow me.
Drop me off at eternity's curb
and I will make things up.
I will make a life for myself.
I will bind the primer of invention.
Motionless already,
I will not know where to stop,
the way Creation
without restraint left Alaska alone.
No further,
higher, lower,
brighter, more perfectly chiseled
or grand?
Out of thin air I produce
a pair of snow geese,
knowing I must be left behind.
And as they glide past
in slow-motion
high speed, their long necks migrate
hours into the future,
where my bicycle
still rests, propped against
the spruce.
Everywhere else glaciers
either inch forward or back.
Matanuska doesn't move.
And if I died here, without you

or you, the ice
would study my bones like a painter
a bowl of apples.
I would never be swept away.

The Source of Every Flame Is Blue

...you wonder why you feel empty
and frown and why goodbyes are hard.
RICHARD HUGO

Summer reminds me, heat
takes a seat easily;
the very sand that scalds

all day, cools
to suit our lovemaking.
You are still on your towel

at daybreak; a thigh
is my pillow, as we are fitted
to a T.

Waking up
in the shallows of the Sound,
you don't swim

but protest, float ideas
of what our future
could be. You wave, ha.

I'm constantly swimming
past you
and getting reeled in.

Pre-Prayer

What else becomes of lovers like us?
The dark is what I saw before I met you.
What I feel when in your arms
is what the divine statutes say
must be heaven before our entrance there,
beauty raised to the power of death.
I hold you because I cannot hold you, nor you me.
Captured spies, we know too much.

Outskirts

When you press your hand
into mine, my pupils dilate,
which gives me night eyes
in the middle of a bright day.
Everything is overexposed:
it's as though the red car, silver
fence, and blue irises
swallowed cans of paint to
supplement their colors
and perspire the overkill
into the air. God,
I'm blind with happiness.
No wonder I can't let go.

'If my pupils could instruct my eyes'

If my pupils could instruct my eyes
to sacrifice color in favor of size,
to expand each black, receiving disc,
I would take the risk.

If I could sensitize my sense of sight
to understand the sense of night,
where shapeless longings are shaded in,
I would accept the sin.

Moods Descending a Staircase

On the first landing,
I'm floored for a second.
Why do moods
overdo it? À la mood,
à la mode, all aboard,
never bored: the finest
moods are not made
from clay but from
the sands of time, blown
into glass and out
of proportion until
they become vessels
of brittle happiness.
The only mood I care
about is yours. Your cirrus
mood that tips the blues
of your eyes with
mischief and cues
my heart's stage manager
to silence the overture
and open your blouse.

We

We're the top tourist attraction in Paris.
We wear sunglasses so people don't tear us
apart. A walking tour of my devotion
to you is offered in no fewer than eleven
languages. We're even stars in Michelin.
People marvel at our architecture,
the beauty of your ribbed vaulting
when you are out of breath with love,
the stained glass windows above
my eyes that color your face when I admire
you. The sightseeing boats, sold out
for weeks, even when it's cold out,
shine their lights in our direction.
And we shine back, exulting.

As God Is Our Coxswain

Your coming is slowing
My coming is going
My coming is knowing
Your coming's tiptoeing
My coming is knowing
This hush will be going
My coming is stowing
Away on your going
And rowing and rowing
Your coming is going
Away and still knowing
Two rivers one flowing
Nowhere and knowing
Yes! and then noing
No! and then sowing
Yes! and then ohing
Your coming is knowing
Melting and snowing
Watered and growing
Our skins are glowing
Our sins are showing
This is holy bestowing

Empirical

As I can fathom neither endlessness
nor the miracle work of deities,
I hypothesize, assume, and guess.

The fact that I love
you and you love me
is all I can prove
and proves me.

Asleep

My young wife's
wings were at rest,
an echo of her body's
ongoing exclamation
of surprise at all
that was beautiful
in the world.
—Or were those
just the sheets,
folded against her
shoulders?
Either way,
she was mortal
suddenly.
Certainly she would
not be troubled,
awake or asleep,
if I reached out
to touch her.
Instead I kept looking
a few moments
longer, to let
the vision linger
in my dreams.

A Winter Wedding

The bride says

In my happiness, the tight
Clench of my eyes, that their lids
Might be sewn shut
Against the sight of time passing.

The groom responds

A descendant of a moth caught
By the light of time passing
In September's porch weather has no thought
Of flight now.

The Bluff

i.

A young man tries to get comfortable
beneath the sheets and comforter after sex
with his wife. The only light is coming
in through the high windows and belongs
next door. He is smiling, perhaps more
than the situation warrants. He makes room
for the cat, who has caught their act from
the end of the bed and now claims a place
among the pillows. The shadows of
bougainvillea give him something to look at.

ii.

Earlier today, doing his best impression
of a stout Cortez, he stood on the bluff
with his *Flowering Plants of the Santa Monica Mountains.*
Unable to make final identification
of what he took to be Bermuda buttercups,
which were glowing in any case
with the fresh memory of record rain,
he stalked more blatant game;
following the author's suggestion,
he crushed a sweet fennel leaf
between his fingers to release an enhanced version
of its signature licorice scent.
I have a crush on humankind, he thinks now,
embracing the mood,
feeling identified and enhanced.

iii.

His line of thought makes
the same nervous forays of the lizard
he saw delivering copy after copy
of sun-news to the shade-dwellers.

As far as emotion, he is in all ways
undecided—much as, this afternoon,
the volume, tone, and balance
of waves and traffic on the contiguous
coast highway a football field
below him were pitched so perfectly
he didn't know whether to be moved
by the recitations of the sea
or repelled by the prose of the passing cars.

iv.

All over town, people are falling asleep
to artificial ocean noise. He cannot tell
whether the sound he falls asleep to
is true love or artificial. The beautiful
woman his body guards along
their shared border is not herself anymore,
or only partly so, as a gala is
in that purgatorial time when the band
has wrapped up for the evening
but there is still laughter.

Young, and Yet a Relic

I try to learn the prose
    of life, but my slavish
Reproduction of its speech
    is wooden; lavish
Praise born of compassionate
    searching is all
I understand. Shall I compare
    thee? Yes.
I liken you to love you,
    to believe the loveliness
Your nakedness displays
    might be proved
By some revealing counterpart,
    might be true.
With metaphors and
    allusions, I feel for you.

II

SEASON OF SÉVERINE

Séverine in Summer School

Naked for twenty-four of our last thirty-six
hours together, and I mean museum-quality, sex-
shop, God-riddling naked, sapping gold
light from the windows of her hundred-year-old
Baltimore dorm, we were hungry for selling
points, like a couple in a showroom. Compelling
arguments were made to close the deal
and children were discussed. I kissed her from heel
to head in a shower without water;
then with. Nude, she read me a letter as a waiter
would his specials, and I couldn't keep
my eyes off: smooth shoulders, belly, pelvis,
deep olive skin all a balm against sleep.
It was from her sexy grandmother in Dieppe
and Séverine translated, both of us
somehow drawn to this third party in a tidal
sort of way, her lunar candor, her antipodal
ease with words and the world. We were difficult,
Séverine and I, a beautiful strain, a cult
of two. Even eating, we made lots of noise.
Even resting in bed, watching the trees,
our lighter breathing, our limb-shifting, sheet-
rustling, even our dreaming had fight.
Her heart was exceptionally loud—not with love,
but with knowing. Knowing what to be afraid of.

Violé

It was like the cartoon dog who accelerates
to break down the door, but the cat waits
behind and opens it when the dog's an inch
away and the dog sails past his lunch
to a far wall and their masters' finest plates.
It was so easy, and silly. And it does not
matter much whether we were dog or cat.

Pre-Raphaelite

We'd be weeds
if trees looked down
but they don't.
We serve the needs
of no one
they know,
and won't.
We water and prune
and scatter seeds
but God knows He
can do that
on his own.
So why do we lie
after love
by the reeds
and feel so very
important?

Sounding Aboard the *Rafaella*

She loved me as the freeloading sea
gulls love the slipstream of a mammoth hull.
It was her passion, this lack of need for me.
She let her resistance fall like an empire, her clothes like a tyrant's
head: momentous and kindling, like no fire since.

And I loved her in the lull
between vessels, in the tenselessness of an unbroken
breaker, in the two mouths where one tongue was spoken.
The freighter's engine throbs against its cage
of ocean, and my heart wrecks against this page.

REX WILDER

Séverine After Dinner

My hand finds the small of his back
and I gauge his response as we dance
to the waves. He caresses my breasts
by invitation, a couplet to offer
the guests, who tonight are the moon,
the moon's lover in the sea,
and the beauty marks of couples
a hundred yards away,
already undercover in my mind.

Séverine in Sunlight

Saints come
briefly to their lives and deaths
in his tears, which about-face
at his eyes and collapse
into the routine of his body
as he makes love to her.
Séverine sees them,
like condensation formed on the inside
panes of a stained glass window,
brilliantly sunlit from behind.

Séverine Between Marriages

Séverine was writing letters
instead of using the telephone.
The snoopy ex-music teacher
across the way probably guessed
suicide.

The sweat beading Séverine's forehead and temples,
though, was not a sign of distress, but of her mind,
at its turning point, letting go.

~

The first months of her thirty-first year
had been spent finding the holes
in arguments, and then looking for something
to fill them with.

~

If you can believe the romances,
Séverine had received the gift
of her physical beauty in installments,
and the instructions had been,
until now, inexplicably withheld.

~

Séverine's letters described in detail plans for her
now unplannable future. They began so energetically

a reader might have thought she'd had a head start,
a page before page one, but then they would peter out, or actually
in, into her next top-heavy attempt to let the world know what
she suddenly didn't.

~

The day Séverine took the bundle of correspondence
to the post office, the walk home took on the significance
of the fall of Rome: all roads led, for once, away.

Higher and lower orders clashed in a series of spontaneous
    demonstrations,
and, with the flourish of an international accord, a sweeping
    lack
of understanding was reached. Impressions, in this new
    atmosphere,
assaulted Séverine like they were trying to sell her something.
The mud scent in the Tuileries, for example, didn't stop at
    wafting;

it badgered her until she, feeling as if she'd just come into a
    good
deal of money, bought the whole park.

~

She took more
and more
showers, especially
on rainy days,
when the steady
stream

that pelted her
felt echoed,
as if all of Paris
were as naked
as she, its every
component,
like a bicycle
spoke, spinning
out delight
in all directions.

~

She loved the way her body
could be so easily slapped
to attention.

~

She opened
her mouth
her arms
her legs

~

...and took the city in. She put the city on.

She put other people in all her places.

She hummed along with ambulances.

She ran her fingers over the slightly oily muscles

of public statues

of famous people

as if she knew them.

~

She ate less meat, and took long walks on the weekends
through the farmlands near her family's country home outside
   of Luneray,
marveling at the damp soil and the touching, week-by-week
   yielding
of innocence on the part of the crops,
especially the Calvados apples and the beautifully strewn

Dieppoise potatoes. Her last weekend in Normandy
she celebrated her birthday with friends and her ex-husband's
   friends,
all of whom noticed the change in her. And although the sound
was drowned out by the popular music on the record player,
Séverine heard ripe fruit fall through stars to the ground.

~

Her rebellion was private,
and consisted in braless,
sprightly walks home from work,
when the most intimate
centrifugal forces could disport
themselves beneath her blouse,
and in wearing short
blue jean skirts sans underwear,

millimeters between the breezes
that touched her and those
that touched the rest of mankind.

~

She couldn't explain it, didn't want to.
Opening the door to her apartment foyer
was as enjoyable as eating a fragrant pastry,
and she would linger at both,
celebrating entrances.

~

Séverine had always slept with nothing on,
but in a fetal position.
Now she woke mornings spread open
like a palm leaf, as if the fan of her own desire.

~

She looked at herself in these moments,
the golden, indeterminate shadows
making their points at every part of her,
and she ran her fingers, as if dialing
an old phone, over the thousands of possible
combinations.

~

Every morning
a new number,
a new response.

Every morning
the same ring
ringing differently
in a new house
that no one had
ever lived in.

~

    Séverine felt
as if
                she were
   sharing
           her body
with a hummingbird
         and
   that all she
   had to do

was relentlessly find flowers.

Séverine at the Albergo Ristorante

An early shower the morning after a storm
and a desperate craving for coffee on the terrace.
Vapors rising from the brilliant lake's surface.
The iron slatted chairs still wet where the wind
blew in the rain from the west. No waiters anywhere.
The earth writing me down like a journal entry,
trying to write me in before I'm out. Me, unbearably
happy. *To love well,* I tell Thirst, my companion,
is to live in mourning for the living. Why bother
with sunrise if not to put the darkness behind us,
to lavish attention on what wakes up, too?

Balcony

i.

Her tongue-traveled-upon torso arches
    inches ahead of the looming
flicker, in praise of it, like a crowd's
    progressive ovation, assuming
the lead runner's arrival; or jasmine,
    anticipating night, blooming—

ii.

If light could slide down your sleeping breasts
    like water, or the moon
dress the bay in sequins... —A mourning dove:
    Too soon, soon, soon.
The perfect note cannot stand on its own.
    Hence memory, the tune.

—Port-la-Galère

Romeo of Séverine

In our most birdlike moments, wings
rarely enter our imaginings.
Perched here, she clings
to me as if I were a branch on the tree
of forever and says things
like "Don't go" and "Stay inside me"
as rivers do to springs
that feed them, and leaving one knee
over her, I hedge temporality.

Le Presbytère

Desperation: no medley or melody, nothing symphonic
    in the pell-mell bird-noise or even mnemonic,
nothing you'd even want to remember for that matter,
    notes pecking at noteworthy, a Satur-
day night university bar scene on a weekday morning
    in a jacaranda tree. Then, without warning,
the flock cleared, perhaps adjoined to the pretty objects
    of their desire; but whether sky or sex,
wanderlust, fawning, or even playfulness lay behind
    the sudden vacancy and silence, I found
your voice there, and talk of breakfast, simple words—
    and was glad to be rid of the pompous birds.

Chaste

Her lips are, well, Impressionist
and forward, and appeared to roam
ever so slightly as the last
sleep left my eyes, while sun
divided monarchies of dust
to humble the silver and gild the toast.
He swore he'd been kissed
when she called him to breakfast
from across the room.

—Arques-la-Bataille

&

Do I have to spell it out? *And* is a grand-
parent or sacred text, respect on demand
certainly, a star on every language's
Hollywood Boulevard, but no teenager's
first choice when heady impatience
walks into the room, her future tense
all beguilement. Eternity's stunt double,
space with impeccable timing, trouble
looked forward to: the ampersand insists
on promiscuity, on strangers' trysts,
no previous likeness necessary until later,
when they get to know each other better.
One line, one pick-up line to prove
no match is inconsequential, or love.

In and Outback

On my back, on her bed.
A lorikeet tipping into guava nectar
by the window was an altar
beneath which she said
nothing for hours with her mouth.
Never been this far south.

Bertolucci Discovers Séverine

Halfway across the   country, the continent
divides, sorting rain   and melting snow,
pronouncing rivers,   filling maps; water's bent
and snapped over   the knee of Colorado.
seeing all, my lust   settles on her still-wet
hair, which parts   easily, and falls into the sun
on one side; on the   other, into none.
Every moment is a   watershed, or not.

Séverine's Ecstasy

I am the tree
in the yard
who can watch
the wood burn
in the fireplace
and do nothing
because I am
a tree in the yard.

Séverine's Neighborhood

Life goes on for some and not for others.
Life goes on for others and not for some.
Some of the others go on with their lives.

Séverine at 85

I was the Speeding Beauty
to your Green Light.
I sped past you without a thought,
on my way to some holy city.

Séverine's Ark

An alarmist mist builds up beyond the zoological park,
Wanting rain from the horizon.
The Victorian architecture is prudish.
The brick is painted navy blue,
And who cannot think of that lonely ship running
Its epoch-making errand for God?

The first time it was because the world was too wild.
The second because there is not wilderness enough.

Inside, a polar bear, contained steam,
Her pelt panted over in a declaration of pure animal,
Lets her cage-mate lift off her slowly—
Not like a ghost, but a ghost's opposite.
She blinks the incandescent light away,
Which catches the future in a dew-drop on his penis.

Lone Figure in a Frozen Landscape

Waves from the Côte d'Azur
break here years later.
After dessert, on the blue
tile floor, her bra was a desert
island surrounded by reefs
of tossed-off summerwear.
The hungry birds who black in
the surface of the frozen
lake peck at the vault
of their prey's heaven.

Séverine and Her Trophy Flower

I was distracted from the roses by an ugly flower.
Actually, by an attractive local who was smelling it.
Stem bent into a letter of introduction. Ill-curled
bloom surprising me with the fragrance of its neglected gasp,
a wholly unrosy odor I could almost devour.
What happened then? Perhaps a quiet, telling rite
of calibration, beauty refining its grasp
on me. I stepped out of my country into the world.

—*Parc Floral des Moutiers*

Normandy Redivivus

I always meant to go back, to loll in salty maritime
Museums sailed through on my inaugural voyage,
To socialize with the local Communists, who have time

To spare, to collect the rewards a boy aged
Thirty promised the man who returned him home,
Which was how it felt, then. Even my marriage,

Terminal, released doses of sweetness, like *les pommes*
Of Calvados and Gourel, into the bloodstream.
Even my broken French healed, churning the foam

Of sympathy. Oh squandered days! A stream
Of scribbled notes drafted in hot fury
And never played. My closed eyes form a seam

About to burst: a scene in which a cherry
Wood writing table opposite a fire
Is magnetic north spreads out from the presbytery

Where we lived, across the barbed wire
That shielded God's half-acre from our Parisian
Neighbors', and over potato fields and a briar

Heath to the castle at Arques and its moat of horizon.
I haunted there, cocksure as Hansel, the ghost
Of a chance, spirit of the chase, racing

Over the greatest possible ground; my heart embossed
With invitations and answers, full beyond reason...
My future, found, had been ordered, and at no cost

To me, to be held under my name (crossed
Out now) until I washed ashore on my native coast:
A shell, into which a new life crawled, almost.

III

IN FULL FLOWER

To a Mermaid

The missionary fog would have all land sea,
and me a fish, or merman, and every tree
salted and buffeted by current. Her grey grace
sways me, admittedly, and some days,
I lean toward the ocean and half-convert,
feeling foreign in the air, and flirt
with the idea of making a life in the ocean.
If only you were here to second the motion.

Rangiressa

I never really saw you until I saw you underwater,
Neptune's hostage, beauty in chains
and just enough red hope in your veins
to struggle, daughter

of gold and the deep. Then after summer
back on land and home,
I sensed, for the first time, the pathetic simmer
of my native clarity, Rome

returned to—which was the easy part.
But I felt the pressure of my neighborhood
and confusion, as if I had to start
over, with a mask and fins. You, by now shiny sand,

threatened through memory's heat
to become the glass my grief hungered
for, an oval, a friend, a coat
stripping all other coats, a guard

at the gate of blindness. But there were bigger
things in winter than love: hospitals
were filled, plazas empty; the rising price of lager
kept us sober, and walls,

walls were built between our cities
by mere boys. Even the warm bath
that let me conjure Rangiressa, its tropic breeze
and child prophet, lacked warmth.

Cows, Bounded on Three Sides by Impenetrable Oak

As far as I can tell, they actively ignore what they hear
or, though this is less likely, don't hear the pleas of the sheer
slash of rock, rigged like a backdrop
at their hindsides, at all. Below, bald sands stop
the immigrating breakers, fitted like bad toupees
to the shore, short of the chalk cliff's white glaze.
I wonder, have the cows always accepted this lack
of alternatives, backs to the wall? Look at them, slack-
jawed and baking happily, half-alive on the lawn.
And yet their cowardice is strangely affecting. I wish upon
their haunches like stars. The appeal of the field is clear.
You must turn away to face it.

Once or twice a year, a cow approaches the cliff, in case it
offers a greener pasture. When she comes near,
she stands where I stand now.
After, the boys and girls from town take away the cow,
or try to, in a kind of game, giggling as they drag and shove
the carcass seaward...

　　　　My dear, be my east, my south, and my north
like a Normandy forest. Bound me on three lovely
sides, and blind me to the fourth, the often lovelier fourth.

　　　　　　　—Varengeville-sur-Mer

Reconciliation, New Mexico

Dusk. A lover's laugh on lover's lane
turns out to be a mourning dove's
brief registration of surprise. The strain
on the silence too great. And it gives.

American Passenger Gold

Sextants were extant when this scene was taking place,
    remember that.
Not that it mattered, there wasn't a star to be seen.
It was another age entirely, as were we all. Our heroine was/is
    Vanessa Gold,
née Kibrick, and let's start with the fact she's dead ahead of time.
But for the time being, she's a cut flower, pretty as could be back
    then,
but daily. Though she sits perfectly still, the sea's heaving
is enacted in miniature on the smooth deck of her breasts.
"Il Cuoco" (Sicilian) has duct-taped condiment holders to the
    sticky tablecloth,
generally battened hatches down for the gale, hurricane,
    apocalypse,
whatever it turns out to be. There are nine levels of heel on this
    tanker;
will everything but the kitchen sink? Father Tom, a retired
    priest
from St. Louis, leads the table in grace. Bearings are what he
    prays for.
Second Mate "Dazha" Danilovic feels his country's soul shaken
by the tempest. Families in city and countryside are sitting
    perfectly
still as their conflicting allegiances are enacted in miniature
on the deck of the *Rafaella*. Two of his children (Ivo, Ljobomir)
will die when the war surprises Split before he does, fearless to
    the last
because Papa would save them, surely Papa. Mama lets the
    Serbs

penetrate her until she rips as if in childbirth in exchange for
    spared
children. Their little skulls bone up on death anyway.
Imagine two uniformed men who keep one-third of their word,
penises back at ease. The ocean will not snap out of its grand mal.
The waves thrash in a loneliness even the ship can feel,
which throws its head down again and again in emphatic,
    sympathetic anger.
Who will hold the sea once it is calm again? No one knows
how we will act in the last moments of life, whether courage
will break through the topsoil of dread like a crocus
or despair cut back mangroves of dignity our sweaty nights have
    bred
from childhood. Dazha, simply, invites Gold to his cabin.
Are you thinking, as I am, that he is also inviting God to his
    cabin?
Neither Dazha nor his guest has any way of knowing
how dramatically peace will be restored aboard the freighter,
that even dowager wannabe Krauss herself, in flowing white,
will be taking the air on the bridge a quarter turn of the globe
from now, with the stern captain murmuring something
under his garlicky breath, and the sun itself riveted on its path
like a Rhodes scholar. In total ignorance then, in Dazha's cell,
with its Italian girlie posters, and strewn dirty clothes, and its
    sentinel lamp
by the shaving mirror, the Second Mate and American
    passenger
Gold, with not so much as a single kiss, undress
and wade into the riptide of his small bunk, where they hold
    each other
perfectly still, and let the motion of the ship carry them to
    paradise.

How He Loved Her

He thought of her as an orange, so he could hold her
roundness in a hand perfectly molded
to her body, and peel her, and feel her sweetness

make a mockery of his tongue, and her citrus voice
glide happily down his throat to his heart.
He planted her like a windbreak of stiff poplars

in the Netherlands, and waited a hundred years
for this multiplication of his desire and his resolve
to reach full height, and then he slalomed

in and out of her like a boy running through a crowd
on a boulevard, so he could know her stillness
observed from the exhilaration of full speed,

so he could be the wind itself that rustled through
her hair, and lifted her generous arms,
which accepted him even as he ran the other way.

He gave her the heft of megalithic
stones and traveled six thousand years backward
to arrange her in lines and semicircles

that no one would understand, so he could watch her
today from an automobile, and be comforted
that she has indeed survived the vicissitudes

of progress, and can, even this far
distanced from him, dull and overshadowed
by gorse and blue jays, move him to tears.

The Sign Says November There

Geese have the long arms of romantic heroes;
they go courting to Canada and back.
And don't we wonder what sustains us,
meat separating from bone in the stew
of time. In the radiance of a naked body,
you can read these words without your glasses:
Cry if you must, but let it be a lover's moan.
If you have to be weak, let it be like a flower-stalk,
which falls on its knees in the rain.

Double Life, California

You're back in Iowa and I wander the canal
in Venice like I'm pacing a terminal,
   waiting to meet you at your gate and make the connecting
flight my imagination arranges. The reflecting
canal could be a runway tonight. Lighted things
seem to taxi or take off. A couple in a window: do they cling
to some hope of their own? The moon I would paint
for you could be the floating lid on the faint
tidal smell here. Let it be daubs
of silver on your August corn, on their green robes.
I think of our robes, on their hangers, in our hotel,
how quietly they make love, and never tell.

IV

THE FIRST FALLING PETALS

Morristown Elegy

I had faith in you. I prayed
to catch every word you said,
like fireflies in the backyard.

Expecting You Home

The front door will open for you like the flap
of an envelope in which an apology card is enclosed.
The oversized pillows, propped against
the headboard like stage mountains, and the cut roses that flank
    them
like nervous producers on opening night
beg the question. The bed's mind is made up.
As we have no children, all I can say is
see how the garden has grown. Zelda, no longer a puppy,
parts the company of delphinium and cosmos
and stops to inspect the calla lilies like a boot camp sergeant.
The latter's leaves, inflated by the late
October wind, swell like chests. The floodlight
over the patio washes over the bird house,
whose inhabitants are never in. The seed sits.
Home is the space every sentence
comes back to. A hundred yards beyond my study window,
headlights throw open the fog's gate and descend on me,
amorphous but so touchingly paired—like a boy and a girl
in a fairy tale.

On the Eve of the Millennium

I put out my only clean pair of socks, not caring
if they match. Although, of course, they do. I drape
tomorrow's plain-colored uniform over the designer
jeans my wife, in Central Park, at the height of her powers
of indiscretion, emptied me out of
and flung, puncturing them, into the recently deflowered

nether-branches of a hawthorn, out of the range
of mortal ears, noses, and naked eyes, but well within
striking distance of the expertly trained Audubon
Society binoculars that day in unfortunate abundance,
making history making love to, and a spectacle
of, me. That was before we heard that time was to be subject

to strict regulations. Now I watch television for hours
on end, and often two or three shows at once.
When something empties, it empties into something.
I opened my rented curtains and let lightlessness
seek, in the glossy surfaces, like a first-time burglar,
restitution, and easier ways out. Herman,

the superintendent from Lisbon, has given notice and gone
to live with his son and daughter-in-law in Jersey. He left me
his non-power tools, the usual ones, plus a dismantled
toaster, which can be made to work again, he said like he was
some psychic healer trying to convince a man
who's had his knees crushed to bone meal: "Don't operate...

concentrate." Right now, I'm shutting out
the world, and thinking about toast. My socks are sopping
wet and I washed them last week. I take the Russian
vodka I bought in West German East Germany out of the freezer
and pour myself some. Suddenly, I am free; or at least
to imagine, which I do. I dive beneath a breaking

wave as clear as this vodka, and come up among splashing
girls, as drunk as I am, but on something purer. Ten years
from today, if you believe statistics, seven percent
will be dead from skin cancer, or some other kind of cancer,
as there are always enough new strains to keep up
with progress and kill the Joneses. The wind crams

like soccer match hooligans through the gap in the window
jamb, which the super no doubt booby-trapped
his last weekend here, when he was fuming Portuguese smoke
signals all over the place, landlord-directed epithets
and the like. *When something empties into something,
the memory of something remains.* My socks, like flabby

sand dabs—to whose existence in this condition I can attest,
but about which I cannot expound, the fish fry in question
happening to belong to a particularly humorless Mafia family
in Queens—discover the muscle of the radiator's grill.
It is, in truth, a hit-or-miss proposition, as the steam heat,
much like my missing Mrs., either sets fires or

puts them out. More often than not, however, I and my socks
freeze on, while my wife, whose gyroscopic breasts blind
people might, with two open palms and a little encouragement,
use to see, as it were, a perfect sunrise and sunset,

or, of course, vice versa, continues to refract the Côte d'Azur
sun with abandon and nothing on, immune to skin cancer

and every other kind of cancer. Her tan, in fact, I hear,
has been making unfair demands on her already insufficient
powers of humility. WOMAN DIVORCES MAN TO MARRY SELF.
Don't laugh. *The memory of something has its own weight,
and can itself be emptied.* At this very moment, if you
believe statistics, a student, to make a point he could never

make at his university, is setting himself on fire.
If he survives, he will no longer be welcome at the café
where he came up with the idea. The newly unsightly
do not, frankly, in a milieu so attuned to the eye, boost
business. I think about visiting the poor
student, at whatever state-run hospital they take him to,

but the irony of the state he was protesting against
now committed, if only by law, to the freedom-lover's speedy
recovery would probably kill him before I got there,
or could even figure out how to send flowers to a country
struggling with democracy. Ten years from today
Jesus Christ will take the place of Greta Garbo,

if only by default, as she will, God granting, be left
alone, at last and for good, thanks to skin cancer,
or some other kind of cancer, and He will be hounded outside
his apartment by the formerly faithless who all of a sudden
want to be his best friend. Look for wienie wagon and knish
concessions, not to mention a lifesize likeness of Himself

on the cross next to John the Baptist, whose head, so
tourists can put in their own and have their picture taken

with the Lord, is missing. *When something empties,*
it empties into something. Every year at this time,
whether or not I'm at a party, I empty the refuse of my life
into a huge plastic bag. I turn to the person next to me

or I turn to the darkness. And it is then I discover
I am no longer holding the huge plastic bag, but am inside
all over again. This will happen ten more times.
If I survive, I expect my wife and the superintendent
to make an appearance on my brownstone stoop,
the latter with fixing my toaster his number one priority

and my wife with an infant in her arms, which she holds out to me.

(31 December 1989)

REX WILDER

The Folder

Folded things speak well of you
when you're out of the room.
They hold the near future captive,
like children about to go on recess
or sexual pleasure at the brim of control.
I think of the pressure of your hand
smoothing over the cloth napkin,
the bedsheet, the piece of clothing—
signals of the meal to come,
the lovemaking, the spent day—
and how you stack the bath towels
as high as they'll go, as a driver
will keep the fuel tank near full
during times of shortage. I step out
of the shower looking to the center
of my life, where you have folded it.
Creases will have nothing to do
with edges: It's no accident
that ledges are ledges and valleys,
so far removed from any real
horizon, where people most often
choose to put down roots and grow.
I like to imagine that God, who,
faced with formlessness, folded
the world into manageable corners,
sent me you to repeat the gesture.

Snails

I love process without progress, a bathtub
filled but never stepped into, a mating
song without expectation. Skills of all kinds
are overrated: The speed of accomplishment
is still speed, a reckless leaving
of things behind... This morning in our house

no one moved. There were shadows at work
behind the drapes like plastic surgeons, giving
our skins new angles to sleep in;
the instruments at our disposal read no future,
no past. Our distances were single cells
in a satisfied beast: this was the house of sloth.

Oh, what failures we were! No bills
were paid, no plants watered, when hungry
we ordered in. We aged a few minutes
every few minutes and night came
as no surprise. Still, it was sad, the passing
of what could not be suspended: your
unimpeachable yawn, my pajama sashay
for the *New York Times*, the samples
of the sixteen perfumes you rubbed
where I'd find them.

The Far Reaches

I pace the beach like a fly
on a ribbon of syrup,
sensitive to air and sweetness.
If I were an ancient Greek,
I'd be wearing armor against
the warrior-god Memory.
The wind, which was easy,
like gentle Zephyrus
that propelled Ulysses close
enough to home
that he stood on the bow
smoothing his clothes
and checking his reflection,
is now two or three winds.
Sand-twisters, gold-flecked,
prove it. In a more
serious time, they could
have been the confounding
north, south, and east
winds, freed when Ulysses'
men opened a sack
in which they expected gold.
But I have no men, only
a woman and three children.
No Odysseys but indolence.
No enemy, curse,
or fatal flaw beyond this love
of light, that travels
everywhere looking for me.

Southernmost Love Poem

The hibiscus that ventures out from under
the banyan tree never looks out of sorts or bloom,
but in fact each rich red affair is a matter of a day
or two at best, a miracle of compression
if not confusion—at once a grand opening gala
and a going-out-of-business sale—
like the thunderstorms that hang out their staticky
laundry beneath the cloudless tropic blue,
or the beautiful red-haired woman who lifts
her skirt hip-high wading out to the rocks,
taking a walk and a swim at the same time,
afraid to miss a thing. Even I, admiring
her grace against the current to the point of tears,
keep the apology that would end our quarrel
straining on its leash. Since perfection is,
among our imperfect kind, no more, I suppose,
than perfect balance, our love leaves nothing
to be desired, only occasionally adjusted for,
the way the wind snaps off fresh blossoms
to make way for a restless procession of buds.

A Sequence of Compromises

1

The cactus adds a wart to give itself a flower.
I dream of such ugliness, of having that power.

2

The hungry fish scale the weedy breakwater ramp
with every wave, glean the greens, and leave their stamp
on me. They dry off to eat; and I, to see, get damp.

3

Every year the leaves compete
to loose themselves onto the street.
I like to think the tree's elite
are those who stay, and take defeat.

4

How, when you touch me, am I dyed without dying?
I hope to undergo your glow forever; or die trying.

5

A narrow bunk found sailors together,
wedging tight against the weather.
When hell broke loose, it was to soften
the edges of our tossing coffin:
I never slept, you never cried—
we crossed the night and never died.

6

One eye is always watering, one eye is perfectly clear.
The latter focuses locally, and on the not-so-near—
the former on what was once, but is no longer, here.

7

Tall cows, short trees—
a weighty question
for the cattle to grapple
with: Do they wait,
unsure, for nature, or prematurely
secure the apple?

8

There's nothing wrong with being right,
said the reconciliation to the fight.

REX WILDER

The Tragedy of Merlin

His Vivien, Lady of the Lake. When
the old magician talked to her he was stalking
himself. Like a boy, he was gawking
at self-discovery's window. Faking
love, he thought. In this he was mistaken.

Meditation in Veules-les-Roses, Dawn

Six thousand years or so into humankind
and lovers are wasting nights still,
littering café sidewalks and casting a spell
broken every morning when sidewalks are cleaned.

V

MORE THORN THAN BLOSSOM

Intermission

The curtain is time's evening wear
at intermission, seducing me like your bare
shoulders, and I stare at the coming hour.

A Double Take

A beautiful sight and I do a double take.
She would like this, I think:
this ibis, or Titian, or lake.

Jealousy

Jealousy is the cat that mews
on either side of the glass.

Innocent

Bliss, like a flower or lover, is meant to be looted.
No thief is guilty who's been recruited.

'dise

Wrenched unripe from the longing tree

Neither sweetness nor softness could be summoned

Even as she remained in the palm of his hand

Regnium Magnus

The gods are forbidden the bodies of mortals,
with a single exception: when pain and oblivion
combine to cloak the union.

Hence Regnium, invisible in full sunlight
on the sidewalk beside the school.
Regnium could not wash the love off his hands

while the woman—a mother? a teacher?—
whose bloody head he cradled
as her seizure settled knew nothing of his desire

but the dark mirror of it that caressed
her awake. They thought she was still shaking
but she was looking where he had gone.

Sapphi

Above this path, at the uppermost boundary
of the untouched land, there's a house.
That's you, all walls and empty spaces
and filled with your own concerns.

The house on the lowermost boundary,
that's me.

In the middle is a spanned, undiminished and undiminishable
    width
without which all longing would collapse.

I'm just a woman
and so are you,
living out our lives in the middle of the middle of recorded time,
suddenly so close to both its beginning and end.
So what are wildflowers to either of us, uncultivated
and uniform in their virginity?

Dinner is served but not before
happiness wrestles me to the ground.

Lonely Man Confronts the World's Problems from His Living Room

Say the woman is not alone, though
you know she is, a single contour
cast by the deflect of neon,
and you are with her in the alley,
though you must watch from
your window, as she climbs the fire
escape the fourth straight night.
Imagine you place your hand
on the woman's splay of shoulders,
tell her, "Don't go tonight."
She stops, but when she turns
around there's no face, only
a mouth pronouncing syllables
like rain against pavement, body
falling against unwilling body.
And when the door opens above
her, there is a stench of whiskey
in the yellow light: pure, welcome.

Lava

With the help of the road, we lifted off the ground
a climate at a time,
leaving the tropics behind and below,
and celebrated the end of the climb
shivering by our truck, so far up we found
six islands to point to.
But the green-glass archipelago
was only the second-best view
of our week together, as top honors go
to this one-room rented
cottage, the scene
of our recidivist crime
against gloom, as seen
from the dented
sofa and the cushion of you,
especially the deft
isolation of that shoe
by the window
overflowing with the time
we have left.

Recessional

When I think of you, you disappear in stages,
as if I were paralyzed below my heart
and wore, like a blanket, a thousand pages
of you on my lap, who come apart
in the slightest wind, and disperse
like leaves. I trade you for the universe,
which holds me back
when I lean over to gather up and restack
your laughter and your temperature.

The more I think of you, the fewer
opportunities remain, as if a painted
memory could not contain you, and you set yourself down in pastel,
fleshed out like a Degas bather—demanding of, yet tainted
by, the light I need to see you well.

And still, what can I do but accept this theft
of woman from man?—until all that is left
is a sadness like unnaked bodies in the dark on a bed,
neither touching nor asleep, and neither comforted.

For S., Whom I Did Not Marry

Turning back the years like the sheets
in the Parc Central, I give the past its due.
That is, its future. We looked down at streets
in one another's arms by the window
as if their lines formed a graph
in which x and y rose together off the page.
Now I offer this epitaph
on a bench beneath a tree that feels my age,
a tupelo, in the middle of Central Park.

Autumn this year is the girl I was good for,
unselfconscious, exquisite, a work
of art at play. On the city's forest floor
lie her love-scene clothes.
She reminds herself of nothing dying,
by the looks of it. So? The throes
of fall have always been death-defying,
the sacrifice of the leaf for the tree.
The leaf built to leave, as she did me.

The Flood

i.

A forest that from drivers' and passengers' points of view
Flourishes four or five states of mind deep turns out,
When viewed from overhead, to be, at best, a moustache
Drawn above each lip of America's parkways and under
Time's nose. No, let's make the metaphor the two
Fingers of a Cub Scout's pledge (the trees) in which
The space that extends beyond the oath
(The unembellished world) is so far removed from hope
That I have to switch images on you again. I'm sorry,
But I'm standing here in the dressing room of my despair
And nothing fits. Still, you must be getting the picture:
Fifty feet to the left and right of the left and right
Shoulder of every drop-dead gorgeous road in creation
And then it's all the moral of the tale. Or look at it
This way: Fewer than a hundred people in Georgia still
Speak with a Southern accent and the salt
Water of sameness is rising in them like a killer tide.

ii.

Let this poem be the helicopter that hovers
Over your alphabetical order. Let the glass bubble be
Large enough for every hurt you've ever endured
As you cruise over every cause and condemn it.
The rotor blades and fuel are my rage and age respectively,
So stopping to re-fuel would mean stopping to re-soul.
I'd rather crash. I do. I'm history. Listen,

Who can take a stand in public anymore without wearing
A politically correct earring of embarrassment?
The nineties are a one-scoop ice cream cone.
What's going on here? A screech of brakes in the cosmos.
Planet Earth at the turn of two thousand's been hit
And is way too hurt to be moved. Wait for the paramedics—
The metaphysics. *Hold me*, the water in every argument cries.

iii.

All I want is a little privacy.
A nature preserve for human nature.
A breeding ground.
A place where God, in peace and quiet, can nurture
A quirk into a mark of distinction, or personality, or art.

iv.

I draw the curtains to bring you the future:
It's just a matter of time before everything touches
Everything and everyone, everyone.
The fortune teller over on Cheshire Bridge is in heaven.
After the flood, she says, angels will arrive,
Less like birds alighting on a wreck
Than vacationers come to partake of (read *plunder*)
Our famous waters. They'll pack their bags
Just as our fates' need to be sealed invokes the cold,
Stay long enough to perform figure-eight
Infinities on the frozen surface, and be off.
So let's hear it for the boy with his finger
In the dike and the international dam industry,
But by no means invest in either.

v.

Tonight, the tender words exchanged
By the two of us in our native language
On this living room sofa would be
The rubber stopper in extinction's sink,
Except that the language itself is full
Of holes. Nuances escape us
Like the animals nobody talks about
Who jumped Noah's ship—and only
Our kisses float on mute reflection.

Cut Memories

I take my memories for the short
term, like cut flowers to be
enjoyed for three or four days,
while still fresh, while not
too receded, and before they become
brown at the edges, and the voices
change, and the hair
assumes the color of the hour,
and the building where
the memory took place is torn down.
I like my memories before
the story of their disappearance
gets old, when you can
still inhale them off your pillow.

Near Affair

To keep our affair near,
I fixed my eyes on the trees
    By the tennis courts
And other rooted
    Things: apartment houses,
Street lamps, the jungle gyms
    Where your children,
Like the breeze-
    Responsive, younger
And frailer limbs
    Of the trees, clashed.
Being adjacent may have
    Substituted
For being embraced, but
    That barely parted
Pair of jacarandas
    Had nothing to prove.
I fell in love with those trees
    And made no move.

VI

WINTER'S FACE

Venice Morning

My head knows you can't stop time
but my heart still tries to freeze things.

My latest fight with myself
(not a fair one, to be sure)
was over a loaf of bread
that you brought as dough
and baked in this very kitchen,
and from which barely three slices
were subtracted at dinner.
I can't very well throw it away now,
can I?

(Like the year that lacked for nothing
save a foreseeable future—
tossed into the catch-all bin
of what might have been.)

Not even bread is eternal.
I make French toast
and the empty plate
is like the face of the forgotten.
More than half a loaf remains
but freezing it mocks
the warmth we once shared.

I guess I'll feed it to the ducks.

Downpour

A rain unprecedented in June,
a monsoon, really,
shakes me from sleep and bed and blows me to the window
and a view of the broken water main
pouring freedom into the starry sky.
A woman once told me a lie like this,
turning everything upside down
but doing nothing to cut the purity of my habit.
You can't start a sentence over
when you get to the last punctuation.

The Clearing

By wearing clothes
to sleep and turning
away on a cold night
you were telling me
you didn't love me
anymore. Morning
came. We touched
through a note you left
by my razor. I ran
into the forest by the
college until I caught
up with my shadow.
Prehistoric boulders
that someone dragged
there, maybe for comic,
even cosmic relief,
welcomed me to what
felt like a battlefield.
What would a plaque
say? Common ground.
Seagulls whitened
an abandoned truck.
Garbage-bones, things
no one used anymore,
covered the meadow.
No flowers. Just pigs.
Big, thick pigs wearing
high-heel slippers,
as if they couldn't

decide between a ball
and a bath. Lonely
hams, tipsy, dusty,
gorging as if the world
were its apple.
None of us can escape
our fate. At least
I can run from mine.

Watching the Boy Watching the Funeral
from the Riverbed

The way this new rain alters
the blood's gravity, making us
wish we'd done certain things
sooner, we can understand
how the field hand's toes
churn the grasses to steady
him, the marsh giving
under to his grief.

The latest betrayal of a body's
pull was the pretty maid who lost
her balance washing stairs
at the Union.
               The boy was known
to love her, but can he make out
the hearse's curtains, the lace
she could have married in? Can
we believe the gossip, that
"just don't get any ideas" were
her last words, and to him?

We can see the sky now teasing
him with promises of last-minute
pardons: clouds tumbling up
like opened eyes, crows
from another town finding
home...

Then a sudden
gust like two hands slapping
from opposite directions, and

just missing.

Drought Notes

Pressure at my temples like a balm to relieve
the pressure that preys beneath it...
Why would anything *want* to be understood?
I loathe not the aftermath but the moment
of comprehension. No more pain
gleaned from the dead run of enlightenment
(where the sails swell but no wind is felt)
than from the ignorant darkness...
That instant, that epiphanic crack is my plague,
and the echoing thud—a code broken,
like a raccoon by a car's headlit prow, and thrown
open for all to see, the spasm, the spine
of unintelligibility thwarted, bent into some
letter of some alphabet. The body of
imminent knowledge, which is all innocent life,
supports its cargo in secrecy, and so naturally
craves the shadows that prolong it.

~

Here lies the lover's lesson, and the rocket
ship's, too, from within whose elaborate
scaffolding the first *I love you* is jettisoned out
of time into space. Flight is black and white,
feet are either firmly planted on the ground
or not. So it was in the beginning, my own
feet very much land-locked and restless
at the state-owned and -operated parking lot's edge...

The freshly painted asphalt surrendered
to the weed-rich red Georgia clay
like a second to a first, more formidable
wife, the one with the kids. The trails,
evidently to weed out the less serious hiker,
were marked blue and red, easier and more
difficult, like arteries and veins in the body

of a spring-wakening forest, but it was
a third branch of trails, one more suited
to goats or death-wishers and marked off
by yellow posts like the faithful who cheer
their wrongly accused and convicted
champion along the road to prison that
decided me.

My seduction had less of Frost to it than Faust.

~

The first days of a drought always pass
like contemporaries of no particular
beauty or distinction who will later become famous,
mobbed and asked for
autographs wherever they go.

~

What lured me to the waterfall was the fall
itself, the sheer serial plunges and dropoffs
even the unrelieved Earth (an inexorable
handicap ramp of a slope to Key West

eight hundred miles away) seemed grateful for
the time, not just to think, but *of* things,
and the warm space such conception requires,
I crave adulterously,
                                and as I proceeded down
the path to my destination, each succeeding
signpost was like a removed garment
tossed at my feet. I came to my senses, which
always seem to be waiting for me in places like this,
as suddenly as if brakes had been applied.
When I stopped, everything that claimed citizenship
to the past, friends, relatives—all my dead,
the illegitimate, legitimizing memories which
had been trailing me and fighting
for position like bicyclists in the draft
of an eighteen-wheeler
truck, surged past me, and disappeared.

~

Dogwoods. Squint and the bract-blossoms
stagger across your liberated vision's plane
like a late city's surviving lit windows.

If every window winds up making light
of whoever draws it blinds, two weeks
from now each flower will abandon

its branch, and illuminate the earth it lands on.

The azalea-scented, dogwood-studded glades
gave way then, like now, to this resort
of ferns, where the youngest members of the oldest
phylum disport themselves with neither
modesty nor motion, their one-piece suits
rolled down to their waists as they soak
in the pine, fir, oak, and tulip-tree shadows
beside what passes, provided I confine
my gaze to the hours between eleven and one,
for a mountain pool. I don't think about
work.

~

A month later, last flower over, summer
beginning to add up. The dogwoods evict us
from the present, only to move us
into a more expensive tense. Denied the beeches'
or the maples' fullness, fulfillment
(June, July, August) eludes them.
They hang out leaves from their foolish
limbs like "Now Leasing" signs.

Drought, too, throws us out, into remembered rain.

~

Days dogged by days, of so little wasted
motion as to suggest winter, and night.

~

REX WILDER

This summer, rain is the romance novel
all nature is reading. Even so, the burgeoning
waist of Angel's Creek (how can it be?)
makes me hope for depth, and life beneath
the surface. Leaves forced to confront
October before Labor Day break down,
making soggy, repeated attempts to assimilate.
Breadth, as if chinning up to a bar,
strains to equal length but cannot contain
itself for long. Beyond the ferns,
beneath the sun, the modest stream pulls
its clouded hood over the hundred-foot plunge
and accelerates in one roared and repeated
word of tribute, beginning in *oh* and ending in
shhh, to the nearby Chattahoochee, so shallow
a city river as never to be bored with praise.

~

"It's only a dog—"
                                A high-pitched sound,
whether the enthusiasm of a startled thing
or the scrape of disparate elements,
any screech that resisted easy identification
(those Chinese firs—behind them—
a halting train?) used to bring
my tragicomic epileptic cocker spaniel Zelda to mind.
She's having another seizure,
I'd think, and tilt my head to calculate
the path my rescue would take.

Now she's gone I rest easy.

~

Where some resort to lopsided risk
to keep their poise in, I make geometry:
My losses, confined, and plotted
along the x axis of my felt history,
free compensation up to wait
along the y and the z, like the same
commuter at opposite ends of the day,
or a meal in the freezer, or a seed.

~

The mathematical improbability staggers me,
that I should be so, on the one hand,
drawn, and on the other, rebuffed by the demands
my loved and living ones make on me,
scattered as they are, their claims on my heart
so unequal, as to have nothing else to do
but loiter here, with not a strain on a muscle.

~

Poise is all I can expect,
when every decision is
a close vote in Parliament
and the contest leaves
both sides' authority in
question.

~

I think of the mind that a monument closes.
A far cry from a Parthenon or even art-deco drive-in,
I echo their sentiments. Spectators arrive in
memory, like days without you. Everything goes as

planned, or doesn't. The architect and inspiration move
on once a monument is up and staying.
"Child." Try saying
that ten thousand years in a row. I'm spending old love.

~

Angela

Awakened by rain, I lay my head
down sideways to meet the rise of her breath
and carefully fall with it,
like foam on a wave, my ear
on the slight swell below
her waist. Heaven has chosen to pitch its next tent here.
I listen in: *Take the heartbeat on faith,*
the gods seem to say, *as only your prayers
will be answered. —Trust the stealth
of the new life inside.* In a sense, it's all over.
The genetic trading floor that decided
the impetuous cell, our son or daughter whom luck
will fit for a century, is empty.

Our family trees are lashed by relief.

Pious

When the snakes came down from the mountains,
we hurried to lock our doors.
Our legs were little comfort,
We slithered 'round the floors.
When our clothes came off we were naked
and our womenfolk were whores.

Screened Porch, Druid Hills

Spring pulls a nervous smile across winter's face.
There has been sweet time taken in the bureaucracy
of the trees, which try to compensate with space.
It's less a filling out, though, than a cover-up—glossy
leaves where brave ones last hung on. Each bract,
each catkin and flower arrives like a gravestone.
No, like a second wife. There's no hiding the fact.
Beauty throws the dog memory a splintering bone.

Family & Fatherhood

Cedars of Lebanon

As a bullet fired at nothing on a desert
will lay its head down ten, twenty miles
away like a poppy's shadow, so my brother
is rumored to have at once come into
and gone out of the world.

I trace the moment
on my mother's face lifetimes later.
What broadcast cheer was born when
the doctors came round with the swaddled news?

Tired as she was, she must
have met them with a smile,
which shivered before it froze.
The same one that greets me to this day.

Eclogue to Nils, 1

You were the secret my parents were going to tell me.
You were the secret my parents were never going to tell me.
You were never lost at sea.
You were never.

Only the full-term stillborn is perfect among God's angels;

Spring, summer, fall.
Without winter at all.

Eclogue to Nils, 2

Sometimes I think of saying to you, "Get a life,"
for a life that was neither started nor ended.
Only you, my flesh and blood,
would not be offended.

Corpus

Souvenir of my mother's time and father's place,
I'm a snow globe now on nobody's shelf;
Mom and Dad have left me to myself,
and the mirror, and two bodies' face.

A Parent Now, Then

I was small, my bed and bedroom large.
Every night my mother appeared
with a glass of ice water, as if to christen

the barge of my going to sleep.
There she was like a movie waiter, precise
and noiseless, setting down my important

drink between the clock and the lamp.
It was no big deal, really.
A small gift, or not even a gift;

a gesture, but not even that. Just a mother,
observant of detail though probably
tired and in need of an hour to herself.

But I was no thirsty sleeper.
In a week I'd probably have a sip
once, maybe twice, before dropping off.

And when I'd wake, or be woken,
the glass still brimmed—or nearly so—
and because of this, graspable time gave way

to the beginning of the remembered. The repeated
gesture hardly bears repeating. Yet for me
it's the blare of a horn on an empty road,

at the moon or even less
than the moon, futile
and wise. To make up for lost time

I'd have to down a reservoir;
to desire what I have no desire for.
But love is seldom assignable.

This is the scene in my head, not less true
for being only imagined:
a woman in her robe at the kitchen sink,

the light of morning a stream
flowing through the Eisenhower windows
into the energized pool of her eyes

as she sizes up the full glass of water
that she tips, then turns upside down.

The Second Conception

There's north, and there's magnetic north.
Seeing the first name Burce on a gravestone in the veterans'
    cemetery,
I wondered if the strange name was owed to the engraver.
Then I found his parents, who did name him, after all.
Here, we never catch up to our own names.
Any time I'm asked my name, I answer
with a moment of my mother and father's time.

Leaping Years

I cannot bear to watch my parents sleeping:
They, unable to keep an eye on me
and I, to keep the company they're keeping.
I imagine them like this, but in each other's arms and weeping,
or laughing, or both, or neither, the night
I broke the surface of the sea.
I let my eyes gloss over them like someone sweeping
a perfectly clean room.
Love spoils, this at least the leaping
years seem to prove, when generations part company;
it cannot keep for our safekeeping.
I cannot bear to watch my parents sleeping.

Pale Grandmother

Jew-meat,
Cossack-prey, shtetl-girl
presses her ruddy
new-

born
into silence's service. Against her breast,
centuries, winters.
Warn

Raisa's
neighbor! Bury everything but the boy
whom my father
replaces.

Rightful Owners

"I'm so happy for you,"
a man said to my wife and me
the day before our son was due.
A small gift, surely.
I barely knew him,
so when he died just two weeks later,
I could lay no claim to grief.
Or could I?
When you step into a great church
for the first time,
do you fall on your knees?
In the nightly reruns of my dreams,
he is not separated
from prayers for my son.

The Key

I'll tell you what responsibility is.
Dusk has defeated Day in a Best of Seven
series, and is advancing to the finals.
My wife won't be home until eleven.

My daughter's in the lifeboat
of her bed, drifting to sleep with her first
grownup book, a paperback about
the *Titanic*. Encouraging my thirst

for pattern and coincidence, ice water
on the nightstand; innocuous bergs bob
in the dark. Cats demand a waiter;
I oblige. Brain and dishwasher throb.

The hunt and capture of the wild boy
is over in ten minutes; as always, he wins
the bottle but loses the war. "Happy day,"
he gurgles between swigs and begins

nodding his head, with a triggered passion,
to starboard and port, as if beating
into the wind of his own anticipation.
Our eyes, meeting and meeting,

say a song, *the* song, is expected
as surely as the weather mark in a regatta.
Profanities run through my head,
fleeing my memory's Torquemada.

I can't sing, never could, am scarred
by more than one music teacher's request
that I "mouth" the words—scared
my rebellious voice would get the best

of the more orderly canaries
in my class. What I would give now
for the throat of a bird, to raise
a tune like a wineglass, to somehow

toast my beautiful son on his birthday
with all the right notes. So what
if he's heard a dozen renditions to die
for already—one after today's haircut,

a barbershop quartet instigated
by a beaming Mom. Faith may not be born
in moments like this, but it
can die, or begin to: the fabric, torn,

unravels, is ruined like a Hardy
heroine. Warm milk shimmers in pink
puddles on his chin. A little Henry
the Eighth. With no more to drink,

he lobs the vessel across the room
and commands me, with his imperious
smile, and sudden silence, to perform.
I launch myself, like a toad for Sirius...

This is what responsibility is:
knowing the right gods and having

them owe you a couple of favors.
Living forty years never craving

them. Surprising only yourself
when a tiny room is immersed
in a miracle of perfect pitch. Half
a minute of song to make hearts burst.

Holiday Special

The Macy's Thanksgiving Day Parade stops
right in front of us, as my wife props
our new baby at her breast to feed.
The printouts on our bracelets read
Monday's date. A daisy on the breakfast tray.
Our window refuses all LA;
it wouldn't open for God. Giant balloons sift
through New York's light rain and lift
the planet ever so slightly, as if cheating
a scale. I'm safe in here, eating
my carryout cafeteria omelette, excused
from work and under a spell induced
by the lack of routine. A backward Proust,
I bask in forgetting my life before today.

Foreword

The infant stands, as if rising
in court to make a motion.
We hurry to hooray, surprising
him, this knish, our Martian

in green pajamas, this Rubens
handful. Handsome in training,
his face's scheduled sense
of style pulls into the station.

What, in clapping, do we wish
for him, or us? At a charity ride
last June, I was at the finish
line, my helmet still on, the side

of the road lined with early
arrivers: we ushered in the late
ones like heroes. He nearly
takes his first step. It can wait,

I think. It's enough, his hand-
over-fist reliance on the table
leg, the blazing ascent
from the cold floor to dabble

in his future, which he wears
lightly, like the world after Rome.
Success closes the course
it rides in on. Buoyed by the sea foam

of our approval, he chins up,
poses, grins—then falls,
dashed against his own hope.
Only slightly daunted, he crawls

away, stretching the moment
behind him like his nation's
flag, gift wrapping the present
in memory and patience.

The Baby

"Doesn't it break your heart,"
 she said to her husband one morning,
"that he's going to die one day?"

The future, until now a silent letter, was pronounced.

The new parents resolved to make
the present a migration toward that
original silence, and vain
progress was made, as if they were rowing
a boat across a lake to a restaurant
they didn't know had closed down.

For Oliver

Now that you have crossed the river
into speech, I welcome you ashore
and salute your open-ended "Da-Da,"
as if the never-say-die
syllable could be repeated forever,
whenever you need me. My fear
is founded in language: that one day
you will say Dad or Father
as if it were nothing and the man you refer
to mortal. Language is a lie.

The First Magnolias

He learned "happy" early for a baby,
a day or two after "apple" and three
before Christmas, on a walk around
the block, and the sweet sound
echoed nothing in our conversation.
It came from far away, like the Asian
magnolias' infant blossoms
that candled ten dozen lawns
and struck me like an annunciation;
in the pronounced synonym for joy,
the father was carried by the boy
on the shoulders of his spontaneity.
Happiness requires no stimulus
at all, or only December's magnolias.

The Racing

You recognize the voice
and you're off
and running with the memory of learning to walk
like dew on your face,
fresh though six months after the fact.
Wild arms steer wilder legs
into revolutionary joy—
you storm the Bastille of your father's crush
on you. If you could only see
your smile: like a loose bow tie.

After-Dinner Sonnet

If wonders vie in the real
world, let this qualify:
the boy has more food
on his plate after his meal.

When it's served to him
the fried rice, broccoli
spears, and teriyaki slices
are flush with the rim

of the bowl; after plowing
through and turning
over the steamy feast,
he leaves the dish overflowing.

Earthlings, mimic this mouth:
Eat up. Cultivate growth.

The Gift

I have no use for your gift
but set it down gingerly
as if the slightest shift
or bobble would bring me
bad luck, or detonate
my love for you. A blade
of grass from an eight-
teen-month old: one day
maybe when you read this,
you'll know what I just
went through. Better yet,
perhaps I'll learn, as
the years pass, what to do
with a blade of grass.

Oliver's Wants

Oliver wants
to cut down
the trees
so birds can sleep
on the ground,
to spend his days
gathering rays
then play
with sunlight
at night.

The War Is Over

At the limits of his imagination,
my son began to show a two-year-old's frustration
at his inability to rouse the sleeping kitten,
who still lay there on the heating pad she wet
in her last moment. Her rib cage
caved in, under fur petted a million times, she was a white
puppet cut from its strings onto a small stage.
Our cat's sense of humor and sight
had expired, but it didn't seem right
or even possible to tell our boy, who would tire
of his exertions before long, we were sure.
Perhaps this is how history begins to be written:
the meeting of spent love and the rage
of a survivor, who tries to kindle another age.

Hollow Pleas

Oliver breathing life into Simon's Dalmatian
from last year. Simon, now the reincarnation
of a *T. rex,* reaching across eras and sibling
rivalry to join hands with his brother. A lemon
moon flooring rooftops: for the first time in
fifty years on Halloween, it was full. "No nibbling
on candy," I intoned, even as I imagined
gorging myself on this evening's too-perfect
peace. Like the handpainted figures on a wind-
up, fairytale Swiss clock, sunny decked-
out neighbors appeared as in response to a chime,
or heralding it. They told us what time
it was. Vampires, ballerinas, superheroes, fairies
trotted out in concert with the World Series.
If anything, the recent tide of events had washed
up more revelers; swells broke and lashed
successive houses with happiness. At one door,
I looked through cottony fog into the score.
A Frankenstein asked, "The game or the war?"
How many townsfolk had his humor killed?
Moribund puns on tombstones filled
whole transformed lawns, and a witch
swept by overhead more like Douglas Fairbanks
than a crone. Addams families stood watch
from the crowded sidewalks, breaking ranks
repeatedly and then regaining them,
the very picture of freedom. The melting pot
of strange flashlights and the reigning beam
of the moon disoriented a Sir Lancelot

and his Powerpuff Girl little sister, who called me
Daddy by mistake. Oliver was appalled. He
wanted up; I lifted the puppy into my arms
as a compass-maker might lower the needle
onto its pivot. Police cars, moved by no alarms,
were tuned to the frequency of need all
the same: they stood for something, like floats
in a New Year's parade, and I was grateful
for their standing, as their penguin fleets
meant reassurance we could use this hateful
October. "Hollow pleas!," Oliver said, waving
his dotty arm at an officer shooting the breeze
by her squad car. (Toddler for "hello police.")
He offered her candy he'd been saving.

Place Mat, with Crayons and Son

Reflected in the sea
of letters is the easy
image. "Moon!" he
repeats until I see
the crescent of the C.

A Half-Hour Epoch

Gesturing with his *T. rex,* he says:
"The allosaurus isn't eated, but I thinked
it." A four-year-old boy in a tub
and his father linked
by morbid thoughts. I read the future
on his puckered hands: extinct.

Before Bed

There's a joke with my son, how the cleanest
thing in the house is the napkin on his lap.
His life is one extended transfer of Best
Foods mayonnaise to Kobe Bryant cap,
peanut butter and jelly on impatient lips
to a sleeve or a swiping back of hand,
mud and grass clippings collected during trips
around the fenced backyard to that banned
lawn of carpet in the master bedroom.
Naturally, as he climbs on me, and off me,
and naps in my arms, his stains become
mine, and my clothes printed with coffee
cake memory-prompts and avocado
salsa that only he enjoyed the first time
around. It is a map I read as I throw
his elaborately dirty clothes, and mine,
less explicit, into the hamper. I follow
the tributary of a chocolate river all the way
to its source, after dinner, in the hollow
of an inverted sugar cone, and call it a day.

The Jungle Ride

In line for the big ride, I was his ride.
He wrapped his arms around
    my waist, stood on my feet and hid
his face against me, riding backward
blind. I saw it all over his head—
    the fake ruins, the spring-break crowd,
and my smile was Nile-wide.
Not until now, to my shame, a decade
    later, do I wonder what *his* face said.

REX WILDER

Morning

Having lost his second pet mouse in a year,
my son cried through the night, encountering
no resistance from darkness.
But morning made a tulip of him,
opening, again, to life.

Police Chase

"Daddy, will you play police chase wif me?
I'll learn you how and then you can write a
poem of it."

—SIMON, AGE 5, AFTER DINNER

I'm on
to Simon
who uses
the Muses
tonight
as bait.
I bite,
and half-
regret
my poetry;
jealous
of Simon,
it steals
me.

Beverly Theatre

I come from a family of forgetters, at least
that's how I remember it, who count on clues
to keep the past intact.
                                So when I found
the carpeted walls, vaulted ceiling
and iridescent chandeliers of that street's last
remembered childhood landmark gone,
a magnificent movie house spread like eraser dust
behind a cordon beside the deli,
it was a small, arcing blow, like static electricity
generated by the heart, and my son
saw the loss register on my face.

He leaned his shoulder against my forearm,
suddenly but lightly, as though adjusting, just so,
a stack of blocks. "They're tearing down
all your memories, Dad," he said,
taking my side against all progress.

Three Lunchboxes

Vaguely military in the predawn light,
three lunchboxes wait to be packed
on the stark and blameless counter.
An empty soul like mine is suited
to the task. I fit sandwiches, trimmed
like sails, into their place, and little bags
of chips, sliced apple canoes, minicartons
of milk. I'm halfway down the fulfillment
feeding chain, and it's time to go.
I hurry the kids to the car,
and they launch themselves into the day.

Jacaranda Squared

After night left us this unremarkable dawn,
our usually voluble son,

mute now like something valuable, cached
himself into a taxi, which rushed

away, complicit. I remained on the side-
walk with a piece of quiet, and stood

awkwardly, as if I had just been handed
a heavy package or, Hemingway-lite, landed

a semi-impressive fish. Two shuffling crows
found me sane enough and allowed me to cross

their path. I joined them, as at a *frites* stand.
"And what brings you out so early, old man?"

the crows, like a chorus, ventured,
pecking at the translucent purple bells absurd-

ly. "My son is fourteen," I explained, as if
that explained it. A crow's life

has different mile markers, so I placed the ache
for them: "His youth is dying of old age.

The toy worshipper and daddy's boy, the humane
snail- and spider-saver cannot take the pain."

An SUV bearing down like truth Tased
us off the philosophical avenue and erased

itself before we knew
what didn't hit us. The lawn, Fitzgerald-blue,

felt adult. "You don't see the point
of things until they're right under your feet."

These the sage last words of the crows.
I picked sticky blooms from between my toes.

Thames Passing

The thrilling helplessness of growing—
you hold the oar but do no rowing
while the secular current keeps you going
and bends in the river keep you from knowing
what's next. On your face, wind is blowing
though no leaves are stirred. Following
you along the bank, parents are doing
their best, running, clumsy and glowing.

for my children

Six-Thirty

I saw a mockingbird in the pepper tree,
and he wasn't mocking.
He just dripped with leftover rain
that looked like sweat.
The rest of the birds sang
seemingly desperately.
This one was dead silent
but alive with suggestion,
distilling the ambient noise.

Myself, I was drowning
in truth-seeking and false starts.
In her bedroom, my daughter
practicing, hoarse with song.
I mimicked the portrait
of a happy family man.

Roxboro Circle

The house you were raised in,
the home you amazed in
was built to last forever,
until you returned with a lover
or a child of your own.
The three gas lamps alone,
survivors of the Civil War,
shone into the future, far
beyond our neighborhood's
circumscribing woods.
The home, I hear, was razed in
haste a year ago or more
along with the circular
block itself: the spokes
of lined trees and walks
and the round park at the center
that was our main square.

for Madeline

Porridge Day

At home among the fixed
and finished, I find inclusive
a questionable virtue and mixed
ingredients impossible to love

anymore. Oh uniqueness, where did
the cinnamon go? I can hard-
ly taste it in this sauce. I died
once when I lost myself in a crowd.

Definition

Under "blind faith" see me
waving to my children
even after I've lost sight of them
behind the tinted windows
and smashed-through tree shadows
of the bending avenue.
The spirit, between assignments,
burrows like a pilot flame.
Even when I'm not waving
I'm waving.

Empty Basket

There was, as her heart saw it,
an element of parole
to her catless exit from the veterinary jail
out into the same sunshine
her pet in his basket,
on his plumped folded clean white towel,
had basked in
only hours before. "It was so pretty,"
she said over the phone,
"I thought he'd like to watch the children
play in the backyard,
and the birds." Now the towel
was all she carried, with the black fur on it,
and the white, which she couldn't see.

Nobade

Since he was a freshly adopted kitten,
he pressured, or allowed, his brothers to do
the dirty work of the morning meow, written
and performed annoyingly by the duo,
in order to expedite the morning feast
for the three of them. Calvin did not waste
away. On the contrary, he made sure
the communal food bowl was licked clean
by matins. His silence defined dawn
for me for years, more than the first gull,
flapping as if to flee the light, or the news-
paper's driveway flop. A fat cat, full
and gliding in a slipstream of duet-mews.
Then Jasper went, and Adam. Two fewer,
the trio collapsed into responsibility:
Calvin sang this morning! *Here's kitty, kitty*
and I thought my heart would break
into the catfood I spooned, the salmon steak
that I portioned unthinkingly for three.

The Weather Never Had Time to Change

We prolong his life only a few days
but oh what days! He meets a vet, stays
overnight with her, learns to walk
all over again and becomes the talk
of her practice. "A tough old
guy," Dr. O tells me the first time,
sold on his release. (Next time, hours cold,
returned in my wife's arms.) I take him home
and the whole night November
comes round with hors d'oeuvres
of hope and calms my shot nerves.
For now we're everything we were.

The Business of Life

REX WILDER

In the Early Days

In the early days, we had to meet everywhere, and often.
Any and all places sufficed to soften
the blow of not being together: Greek coffee
shops downtown or cafés on Columbus; at the Y
after readings; on the subway and in parks;
on street corners and front stoops; on larks
and tangents, like that heron-rich train trip
upriver to Schenectady. Seven
days a week, we were filling up the tank of our friendship.
It was wasteful like any heaven
and eventually the intimacies we exchanged
drew us so close, we grew deranged
with self-knowledge. In the end, I knew you no better
and myself too well, the way q knows the letter
u. You moved and I took my cue
to return to Los Angeles, to let the years renew
us, until we were a different
vehicle altogether—still made for transport, but efficient:
Now kingdoms cropped up from a handful of words
scrawled across the back of museum postcards
or spoken into a receiver. To wit, tonight: once your time zone
reclaims you, I'm awake with
whatever it is that loathes annihilation, perhaps the myth
of union itself. Instead of this silence,
we'd still be talking, in the early days, running
through details like Pamplona
bulls until one of us died, or fell asleep mid-sentence.

From *The Clear Coast*

We went into the ripe woods by the sea
with metal buckets to collect guilt.
The vegetation was low, thick, sure of itself,
into itself, a vain forest—yet the pines
appeared deferential, and said a prayer
for us as we passed. Why, then, guilt?
Because it was, since you asked,
what this wild land was bursting with.
Was obsessed with, the way a child,
learning his letters, sees *x*'s, *s*'s, and *o*'s
on the backs of beetles, in the patterns
of spilled toys, and in varicose veins.
Guilt ornamenting thicket, bramble, ivy.
It was guilt in berries' clothing, guilty
as sin from the summer, that left us
in a lather, as we plucked and foraged
away. We took turns forgetting
to set the parking brake, cover the pool,
and lock up the poison, then neglected
our loved ones in rapid fire.
We cheered each other on, since none
of us was perfect. We didn't feel
like predators—yet who of us so much
as loosened our hold on that creaky
handle as we walked home in the dark,
swinging our buckets of juicy guilt?
We had a lot to be sorry for, and tipped
our guide accordingly.

The Second Floor

After nearly a year of hearing
   false rain play while we lay,
eyes closed and posing for
   a blissful death—the real thing:
nature's paean to restraint,
   the always measured display
of sound at its shallowest,
   as Heaven and Earth sing.

So much was make-believe
   in that studio where we practiced
Eastern thinking above
   an Italian bistro in West LA
that this shred of authenticity
   was welcome artifice:
the perspiration of perfection,
   God trying, a roundelay.

Even the instructor seemed
   to appreciate the opportunity;
he turned off the expensive
   sound system and steered
his savasana patter to the end
   of the drought. Our pretty
bodies were an echo of the rain
   drops, as we disappeared.

The Six O'Clock

In a class of seventy, I was the only one blinded:

The low sun poured through two small windows,

as if itself relaxing in corpse or savasana pose,

while we unwound and were hardly winded.

All were wide-eyed except for me. Not that I minded

serving as shield and decoy for rows and rows

of devotees. For a while, I was the setting

sun's pet; I gave as much light as I was getting.

The Funny Farm

In the calm that survived the storm
a puddle in an upside-down hat
presented a world to me in which this is that,
memory is the manure we grow out of,
and fate the fake we expose with love.

Two Nights of Stars

Seen from home, they chart a precipitous
decline, in a heartbeat or net worth;
or to the optimist, an overnight success.
Shaping up for "the ends of the earth,"
as the ad says, a charity bicycle ride.
I kill myself on the cliff stairs, under
the stars, looking three steps ahead
and one breath, as my senses wander.
The rats in the weedy shadows eagerly
follow my progress: a golf match gallery.
The moon, or a monster streetlight
above the eucalyptus, limns my flight.
Seen from home... but I'm nowhere close
to that middle earth, the lost cause.

In New Hampshire

A warped, wounded screen.
The crenellated drapes
moldy, the windows open.
In the dense air of too
much, lightning followed by no
thunder but raindrops
audible on leaves.
I remember old loves.

Trout Sky

Of course you can't see your feet and can only feel
what your feet see, the uneven, pebbled, grassy
      dirt, when you walk out to the lake at night to fall
in love. From the calm, you'd expect a glassy
surface to reflect the heavens and a distant birdcall
      to surprise you with a whisper's intimacy
at least once or twice before you return to the world.

But Lilliputian waves gulliver the senses: they bully
mirror and hearer both until your only choice
      is to recognize their authority. They're almost silly,
as they invisibly sidle and sully, but to chase
them away you'd have to be the moon. What is fully
      there? Only the Jeffrey pines, their chaise
longue languor spelled out in butterscotch letters.

René Underground

So the angel, accustomed to, and long ago fed up with, his
    taxing
and unromantic reliance on wings, lost track of time
burrowing beneath the unstable clay, cavorting, if you will,
with the indigenous gophers. This is easy to imagine.
If you received an invitation signed in the unmistakable scrawl
of an owl one evening, would you say no to his offer
of a fully chaperoned and (with any luck) bloodless high-altitude
    mousing,
even though you had a hundred and one chores
to do around the house? The yuccas, who would later surprise
the whole of Malibu Canyon with their sudden burst into
    prominence
the weekend before the Independence Day holidays, courtesy
of a not-as-ashamed-as-he-should-have-been
angel whose job it had been (and still was!) to push
their candelabra-like stalks into the sky and paper them with
    flowers
that always turned out to be miniature versions
of his wings in moonlight—the yuccas, who were called by
    postcard writers
"Our Lord's Candles" for the way they looked
when the flame of their flower was highest and for the way they
    flowered
just before the flame was snuffed and the yucca died—
the yuccas, like it or not, were out of luck,
and would have, until the charms of the underground wore off
for the angel, or he was bitten by a rattlesnake, or the urge

for a breath of fresh air, to wait. For now, he savored the
     difficulty
of movement, the drag of the laurel sumac roots on his ailerons,
the brownness deeper than any lack of light
that could not but overwhelm him who was bored to tears
with the lacy, doily life of an angel and the adjectives
assigned to him as part of his job that were never very far from
     "opalescent"...
The crawling made him dream. The creeping made him weep.
He didn't care that his wings were tattered
like clouds breaking up after a storm, that his mouth full of
     poetry
was breathless with broken-up rock and unrealized seed.
He had often secretly prayed to gophers. He was kissing one now.

Amphibia

We crawl onto land every day,
though the air isn't right
and the light refuses to waver.
Our wake, the water.
We call this longing *dance*.
Oh the grace of that woman
climbing the stairs!
Take me to her lily pad!
At work, we bury
the future; home, we honor
the dead. Our aim is true,
as it always has been.
We crawl onto land every day.

Hard to Say

"Tell me, is the more-or-less moth facing
    up, gazing at night sky through vines,
or down, to the sidewalk snails are pacing
    with their aimless trails and artless designs?
Lit from beneath or above by the horizontal
    desk light, is it basking,
stiller than a girl by a pool who wants all
    the sun to herself, asking
nothing of the window other than purchase?
    Is it the picture of mental hurt or health,
balanced gamely between the desire to chase
    annihilating heat and the wealth
of knowledge explaining the vanity therein?"

I was staring at the glass, past my face
and a furred reflection of the kitchen,
before this ambiguity landed like a shred of lace
blown from some dreamy venue,
and I will be longing still in its ghostly wake,
loving false and loyal to true—
torn in two for wholeness' sake.

Valentino

Against the Eden green and the densities of the avocados,
high and impenetrable as planets, against a blue like Cádiz,
in the uninflected coast light and the light violet
haze of their fellow June recruits, jacaranda blooms lit
on falling branches of air. One or two a minute,
as if they were receiving diplomas. Because the prevailing
westerlies were quiet (it was no day for sailing),
the blossoms fell as obediently as shadows or rain
and formed a purple picture of the tree on the lawn.
Bees with the coloring of tigers seen through train
windows pawed the soft Victorian bells. I lay on the grass
and the grass carried me, as if my body were Cleopatra's.

In Danger,   The Shallows

He's bold, or dead:

        those are my first two guesses.

He resists or doesn't resist

        my advances,

that's for sure, like a skin of ice,

        or the bucket of a marriage.

What do you expect,

        at my age—

that I would let anything

        so blatant as love

languish there?

        He has the bearing of a lodge,

somehow, though he is only

        a monk seal,

rare or rarer. For the first time

        in my life, there is nowhere to fall.

He lifts his simian head

        and caresses the spray;

Whiskers paddle his funny face.

        "Nothing," I say.

Model Model

On the platform, at the art school,
without clothes to frame me.
The students seem impressed—up
and down they eye me
from behind their easels.
I have never felt so dressed up.

Starstruck

Tonight, stars drain out of the zodiac.
They beseech me, devastating me with holes, unslaked
vacancies. I am not in my body when I am most myself.
Every imperfection—or wrecked perfection,
every unbalanced cheekbone, street, or tree,
every less-than-lovely laugh
or quaking earth is proof I have been breaking
and entering. The wind from the sea
spins my midnight pores, elevating an unabated
aching: I want nothing I cannot take part in.

—Theoule-sur-Mer

REX WILDER

Where the Frogs Unfold

At the hour when stars fold
themselves up in the
colors of day, on the corner
where the frogs unfold,
dawn dismantles a
lingering fog.

In the window where you stand
your breath erases this
corner view with laughter:
Are frogs fools to cross
the street? Is the mud warmer
or mates more receptive?

Each green belly treads black
earth across the street.
With every clumsy jump, a puff
of steam tumbles treeward,
cloudward, toward the hidden
folds of suns hundreds, millions
of years away. This is the path
of your memory: your daughter
dead in her sleep last summer,
your husband since gone mad.

When you open the window,
you find only more possibilities:
the last croaks floating,
rising and losing volume as

their inspiration sinks
into the marsh; the odd rustle
at the grasses' edge
that always turns out
to be the patter of friends'
children.

Falling Through the Light

I'm not alone or
even close when I return to the shore
at five and wait
for the sun to differentiate
Jeffreys from Ponderosas. It's always autumn at this hour,
when we discover who we are
courtesy of the most impersonal power.

—*Big Bear Lake*

'With the sun midway'

With the sun midway
across the heavens on a summer's day
   at Vezin and pleasure
   craft taking their leisure
a little too seriously—not even the parasailer wavers—
forgive me if I say
     the lighting does no one any favors
     with its blunt and aimless beat
that makes us look artificially incomplete
and insanely same.
   Shadows seem halfhearted in their claim.
   Not even the two rock
islands make the short list of the scenically elite
     at twelve or one o'clock.
     To love now would be to ignore
what's inside and what's in store.

Polynesiac

Sink, I said, trying
to submerge myself
a human's height
beneath the surface;
managed a moment,
achieving parity
with the parrotfish,
who let me gawk,
as if this turquoise
room were the stage
of a gentlemen's
club. Breathless,
I turned a shade of
blue myself, or so
the pretty panic felt.
Then once again
the dry world had
my back, and I
floated like the corpse
of ambition, shot
down from shallow
heaven. We never
quite belong because
we always nearly
belong: this, the Zen
of the denizens
of the deep. Sink,
I said, at ease
again, after clearing

water and air from
my snorkel. And
down I went, another
forty times at least,
relentless dissenter,
to meet my
uncomfortable fate.

Villainelle

There's been a mistake. You're free to go. Be well.
Return to the world of light, see your hands again.
Vary your exit times. Avoid the rush from hell.

Turns out the plaintiffs had your evil spell
Coming. Your crime covered theirs; sin cleanses sin.
There's been a mistake. You're free to go. Be well.

There's bound to be a backup; security personnel
Are undertrained and emotional to a man.
Vary your exit times. Avoid the rush. Hell,

I'm choked up myself. I like you. You're real.
It hasn't been so bad, has it? Always a fire to fan,
At least. You're free to go. Be well,

My friends. Think of us here where first you fell,
Murder-fresh and cradling your weapon.
Vary your exit times. Avoid the rush from hell.

Remember the beauty in the soft swell
Of a wrong's grave; virtue has its day in the sun.
It's not a mistake. You're free to go. Be well.
Vary your exit times. Avoid the rush from hell.

Agave Marginata

If you've never seen an agave, imagine the tentacles of an oc-
topus, washed ashore, and then torn by the sun from the rock,
or, better, arms turned Godward around the scene of an
    accident.
The tourists took it for a cactus, making the ascent
to its porphyry cliff, but for the view from there;
the agave, like a silent letter, was attentively ignored.
Then one day, or year, yielded a reward
equal to a lifetime in which no one seemed to care.
The succulent grew ugly, paling as the last-minute tolls
    were paid.
Yet I was heartened: the plant, having lived horizontally
so quietly, would now become a tree.
Emerging from the frayed
covert of leaves, the flower took the sky by storm
and was the agave's final form.

REX WILDER

The New Life

I stand on hollow ground outside the gates
of Grace Church in light rain, which sinks
into the deep prayer of the lawn. The rain hates
me for my raincoat. The white sky states
the obvious. Nothing, like anything, awaits.

On Martha's Vineyard

The islanders travel well below the island's
posted speed limit. I tailgate in silence,
making myself known but growing more inclined to slow
as I think how my life's pursuit of so-and-so
is like these cars on their circular roads
who, when they arrive to drop off their necessary loads
of groceries or half-naked bathers, do so knowing
they're where they started when they get where they're going.
But what am I saying? I want what I want.
Pointless as it is, it is where I'm pointing. Why linger?
Neither the encroaching pines nor approaching blind curves daunt
me: I pass three cars, shy neither with horn nor finger.

REX WILDER

Waiting for Clearance

Winter, and this cornered remnant of pine forest
seems to have no interest
in mounting a stand, in keeping out what's best
for the city. Tall as ever, unbent,
still the trees sense, or ought to, the pervasiveness
of their abandonment.
Look! Not even the sun will pay rent
on this property, its time now spent
shadowing balconies and towers—
not even the sun will invest
in spring. Like anyone oppressed,
the trees would pack up and move on with a sigh
but for the one oak with the high
and wide outstretched arms, holding the rest
back—or so the oak brags to passersby.

Local Beauty

We should all live on Hill Street, with its human rise and length,
that begins in general (a general store) and ends on the strength
of a dead end, that barrier from which no surprise
ever advances. Nearby, a river, a forest, a farm, unlimited supplies
for anyone hungering for the picturesque;
even the local beauty, if you're lucky, at her writing desk,
autumn-haired in the yellow house. There she is! A friend
is coming to visit whom she does not want to send
away disappointed, and she's making out a list of things to do.
Vehemently, she draws a line through
an idea that seemed great only yesterday. Such an effort to please!
May she never be crossed out vehemently herself and pleas
like it are heard and ignored by those who sit in judgment:
    the ritual
black coffee, the blind cat's chair, the books on the windowsill.

Wisconsin Avenue, Georgetown

It's the graceful bodies we won't let go of,
the historic landmarks we protect.
      The stores themselves are shallow souls that love
us for our money and do not remember the architect.

Frozen Food for Thought

Aisles of confined scents and guarded promises.
Cacciatores, low-cal entrees, somebody's grandmother's pies
say time can be saved—a white lie

our better selves cook uncovered in a microwave
until just done.
There's an air of immortality about your grocer's freezer,

or at least of outlandish patience.
Sweet peas fresh-frozen in August await
the prince's kiss.

Echo, Echo!

Today, late
May, late me.
Romance
Streams, runnels
Of desire driving

Our sainted
Chaparral
Insane. I too
Was green once
And will be again.

Parity Island

Garibaldi, encelia, casino, cove,
kelp-bed, Catalina cherry, blue—
when every noun around you
achieves synonym status with love,
there's nowhere deeper to dive
than the shallows they sell to the tourists
or more healing than the salve
of Here, where nothing persists.

Grandpresents

Languorous in the semi-shade of the pear,
a canopy of blossoms crowding leaves
at least five seasons old, grandparents dare
grandchildren to shoot, as each cleaves
to the love of basketball, or any game
or gambit that brings loved ones home.

Time glows in dunks, banks, fallaways,
swishes, no-look passes and alley-oops,
and, in the fans' hourglass, attaboys
and voluble cheers extend the boys' hoops
at least an hour. Only the assimilated
parrots in the silk tree see the day repeated.

Silencing the Yard

When I walk out the front door and down
the gravel path to the mailbox or the paper,
I am confronted by my garden, which has
always been critical. "What do you see in her?"
the aggressive hydrangeas demand, perhaps
cranky with the drought and my forgetfulness
with the watering can. "She's so loud,"
the three oak trees lined up at the edge
of the property whisper with their shadows.
Wildflowers, which you have called weeds
right in front of their faces, think you think
you're better than the rest of the world.
Well, you are. Let's start there. You are.
Just once I would like to rip your critics
up from their roots, drag them
gasping across the threshold of our house
and teach them a thing or two about love.
But who am I kidding? My hands are full.

The Joy Thief

He was the last of the great romantic mopes.
He walked in a cloud, perhaps in hopes
of soaking up sky and becoming more blue,
but bowed to green as a needier hue:
he was a connoisseur of gardens, an editor
of colors who changed nothing of
his authors' works, content to love.
I see him now, gaping at the new
shoots, the unlit bulbs, the fragile impatiens,
as if he were the garden fence
itself, keeping out the impatient predator
deer and rodent. If he had anything to
bequeath from this life, it was innocence,
though by now his heirs are gone, too.

The Space of Ten Dozen Lawns

At last the kids are grown, away at X
university or making Y city their own.
There's a For Sale sign on your lawn.
Will you or will you not welcome
the fresh parents still smelling of sex?

Dark and Lonely Street

The sight of families in retreat,
now distant enough to look like cut-out silhouettes
one piled on the other,
assaults me so with loneliness that consoling
memories are called up like the National Guard,
fragments difficult as fresh-fallen powder
to fashion into a useful whole—
vague recombinations of happy vows, retired goals,
phantom friends, wavering landmarks.
Then the memory-ball crumbles, as it always does:
I'm the prodigal heir to a giant chain of last resorts.

How soon what matters is leveled out and sinks to indifference!
Already the ocean of Oglethorpe Avenue looms.
As two or three fireflies hang back like non-swimmers
on a dock, I push off into the painful noise
and glare, where I paddle now, among strangers,
introducing myself.

Totalitarian Memory Poem

I came a long way and stayed in castles.
I'm on top of the Berlin Wall. A soldier hustles
through the guarded Eden at my feet:
Does he want to join me or shoot
me? It's sunset, and the colors don't compare
to the concentrated freedom in the air.

The Business of Life

I love to walk, block after block, granting distance
to the cramped, sped-past neighborhood.
I love to look, from the yard with the white picket fence
to the fenceless one with the stacked wood,
creating a mythology that's true
for seventeen-twenty-four and seventeen-thirty-two.

I love to note, and nod, and notice
the predisposition of the voters,
how the Democratic placards go
with fussy lawns, while Republicans sow
the seeds of carefree enterprise.

I love to walk, block after block, taking steps
left by God or the city planner for citizens
such as myself to take, and making stops
as well, like the fallen leaves of light, tens
of thousands of them, that day and night rake
and remove. I walk and look to have a stake

in the business of life, and not just be
the taker of givens, its employee.

The Sad Divides

Between work and work dinner on a business trip
in a walking town and late already, I duck off Peachtree Boulevard,
the direct route, and glide onto Something Lane,
where I submit almost instantly, dreamily, to a spell of safety
three dozen stately homes long.
The street seems blessedly drained of events.
Magnolia blossoms breathe sigh after sigh of relief,
the air conditioners drone.
I grow into my imagination.
A washed car steams in its puddled driveway.
Lighted windows broadcast the evening anchors, silenced.
The sad divides.

Fire Ant

By my own rules
do I measure,
my own jewels
do I treasure.

I find my peace
among the galaxies:
when I exclude,
I find my magnitude.

I am a fire ant.
I am ignorant,
primitive, brass,
an insect king:

I do the electing.
I'm the picture of languor
beneath your
magnifying glass.

The Hollywood Reporter

In Los Angeles, the palms audition for the part
of you. Cars admire from the freeways

but, like me, they have no say. Waiters dart
among sunny tables, and act for free in plays.

The husband does what the wife says.
There's order in Los Angeles, and laws

prohibiting nudity on Malibu Beach.
Palms stay palms, though they reach and reach.

Work Weather

The whispers hardly stay whispers.
The boss has just passed, like a summer storm,
or in some way passed them over.
Disgruntled atoms are drawn
into molecules of gossip—
who can resist the drama?
Look at me jumping into the puddles
of heightened chat, splashing
their market mortality onto the endless day.

Red Light

Virtuous behind the wheel,
he prides himself on the urban patience
the motorists behind him
don't display. Rex, Rex,
there he doesn't go again:
He's sitting at a stop sign,
waiting for the light to change.

Work Faces

A bouquet of work faces presented
each morning, seemingly for the effort
of my commute, a zoo of expressions
trotted out for meetings and fed
by keepers for the benefit of millions.

Work faces are catalogued by rumor:
in Atlanta, they are distinguished by
an air of mock invitation and mint julep;
in New York, high expectations bend
smiles into the sunlight of paychecks.

Work faces! Drafted into service by love
and bills, bullied into usefulness
like a shopping cart with one jammed wheel.

Forgive them.

Acacionally

The acacia stands out from the dull live
oaks and scraggly walnuts like a dictator
on a balcony, a ridiculously impressive
hue doing a number on me, the spectator
and commuter. We the cynics worry
too much about the distributors of glory,
even as we bask in it, and try to matter.

Empty Hands

Friends moan about what they've lost:
love, opportunities, longed-for, hard-earned.
I grieve for what I've found
and, greedy for reward, returned.

Song for Renée Fleming

Whether I'm in Iceland with friends or Rome for work,
the lights on 38th Street balconies beckon—
I book my ticket back. I can't miss Christmas in New York.

I'm a busy woman, my calendar is brimming
like an ice cube tray in the humming freezer.
But let the food carts know—your regular is coming!

I can't miss Christmas in New York. Which rink
isn't my favorite, I smile to myself, longing to glide
the frozen puddles. A million trees blink

at me in December, as if I said something witty.
Old friends, let's stroll Fifth Avenue arm in arm, with presents!
I can't miss Christmas in New York City.

Touching down at Kennedy feels like shoes
traded for slippers. I have followed my dreams,
but dreams of home stay with me like secret tattoos.

Snow will fall tonight, or fail to—both ways work
to soothe me, as the taxi ribbons through the park.
I can't miss Christmas: I'm in New York.

The Last Ten Minutes

I am the greatest nation on earth and into me melt
A hundred epochs of ice, the calming skin of the water come to
    rest
In a motionless glass, water that will, when swallowed,
Make my own flesh a kind of interior
And demand of the air in the room and the buildings across the
    street
And the swaths of forests coursing like rivers
Between former forests and the rivers themselves that they be
My heart and my head. I am the greatest nation on earth and
    into me melts
The smell of the rose on the table whose display was delayed
Until after its move from soil to vase—a rose I removed from
    the earth
Of which I am, by virtue of style, the greatest nation.
The sky will soon apply inside me for permission to proceed.
Birds (read *impressions made*) will move
Stage left to right in iambs past my setting sun,
Blue as veins coming, red as arteries going,
The sole but substantial wind created by their alternating *m, v,*
    m, v, m, v,
Though those letters too will collapse in the absence of vowels
(Read *soul*), to be replaced by draftless gliding parallel
    continuous lines.
The white space time cannot black in or out
Is how these lines hold sway. Into me melts the mind of the
    water
On the lip of the glass that chaperones the poison.

Thick, deliberate, irreversible, the mind of the water conducts
    my thoughts
Like the last ferry of the season on a northern lake.
I show my gratitude by dying before I reach the other side.
May my successors enjoy the circuitous winter detour.

Slow

Slow, I get in the Christmas mood
early in January. I wade in behind the tide
of events, on time's dry sand.
In this, there seems to be some good:
My view's unique; beyond the end,
the sky itself gets off the ground.
I take the past by surprise, and goad
the resigned beast with renewed
currency. Lived life is always sold
half-off, cleared out, paid
far less than full attention to. Sad,
yes, but I fill in like a god,
with praise. This is how I get ahead:
by standing firm and falling behind.

Forty-Two Below

A few of us gather to root for the newborn calf—
the awkward splay of its landing gear,
its coat lathered and almost geologically steaming.
You'd swear the animal purrs.
Under care in this torch-warmed garage,
the calf made it here alive by luck,
the farmer having been able to dislodge
it, before his patience waned, from the ice-drift
and the parent. How many living things
cry out on the brightest afternoon?
How can such obvious pain be so barely apparent?
We are too widely strewn ourselves
to count on anybody's help, to hope that we'll
be found in time. And so we celebrate the rare
survivor, even as clouds fill in blue
holes above the mesas ten miles behind the two-
block town, like silver dirt
shoveled into the sky from nowhere.

REX WILDER

Snow

i.

Stray memories landed on top of our car
overnight, weighted by nothing but the desire
to be recollected, and collected, here this once
upon a time in the mountains.

ii.

We scraped the windows and lumbered, chained,
down thousands of feet to where it rained.
Shaken snow lifted off the hood and mirrors
like jets from carriers.

Rain / Storm

The drought-ending flood
bears down on us
and all we can think of
is clinging to the hill.

Fall / Light

To die, she told me,
is to fill with mortal light,
as when a hand opens
and loses hold.

Boomerangs

Crow)

Crow!
Crushed under my tires.
And *now* I
slow...

Wishes)

Wishes
are best kept loose. To wit, the gallinule's
hues—when I came for
the fishes'.

Wasted)

Wasted
display pastries make me want to get out
more—to be inhaled, handled,
and tasted.

Pigeon)

Pigeon,
poor pigeon, trying to kill
himself by jumping off
the bridge.

Fishing)

Fishing
pole love poem: we reel in
one punctured
wish.

Weird)

Weird
white flies buzz the face of the old
hibiscus, ghosting
a beard.

How)

How do
you know when an old soul comes of age?
Does wisdom collect what years
endow?

How)

How
to put food on the table,
the cleaver asked
the cow.

Cherry)

Cherry
blossoms rain and fill the branches'
reflection, plentiful and
plenipotentiary.

Love)

Love
breaks against dawn's shore until
no bed is wide
enough.

Rented)

Rented,
our lives are rented. Return
delighted-in, and
dented.

Some)

Some
view! Press me into it; ask
the camera to be
a thumb.

Stories)

Stories
told make you old, they
say, the morning
glories.

Raj)

Raj's
first American New Year—neither
a welcome home nor a bon
voyage.

Old)

Old
people steady parents in temple;
they still do what
they're told.

Views)

Views
have no close relatives, only jealous
neighbors and a whorish
muse.

Forced)

Forced on her
like a pickle by Sandwich Sam (not
his name): leaky promises.
Divorced.

Insulted)

Insulted
the office to pay compliments outside:
surfaces glowed, souls
exulted.

Embassy)

Embassy
flags flag; the wind blows
right through
them.

Under)

Under ten,
they're still asking questions;
ten, it's over, the automatic
wonder.

Girls)

Girls
change into prom dresses, or *in* them,
and limo doors open
for pearls.

Heretical)

Heretical
magnolias emblazon the sky above.
For us, their perfume is
theoretical.

Who)

Who
doesn't try to keep the hunter
happy? It's easy meat
at the zoo.

Preparing)

Preparing
lunches for money—the touching
simulacrum of
caring.

Fairness)

Fairness
fouled: a beautiful seabird
not rescued because
not rare.

Outrage)

Outrage
loves the conspicuous absence:
a pumpkin sage lasagna
without sage.

Major)

Major
literary event—blowhard! Sure,
I'd read it, if I lost
a wager.

Fearsome)

Fearsome
cliché: "Moderation in Everything" is bandied
immoderately, including
here.

Paraphrase)

"Paraphrase"
(of all words) runs off like a cat;
doesn't return for
four days.

Here's)

Here's
a forest at the farmers' market:
a tidy stand of asparagus
spears.

Glass)

Glass
bottom tickling the kelp is glass
top to the dreamy
bass.

Waiting)

Waiting
for a humpback to leap—
the sun and a sailboat
baiting.

Beds)

Beds,
pillows—religions? Tithe our
bodies' prayers and tired
heads.

Rushflowers)

Rushflowers—
the lovely, blowsy, grounded
camellias are suicide's
brochures.

Silo)

Silo country,
Venus-poor—and me dreaming,
mile after de
Milo.

Parked)

Parked
on a bench as the ranger Distance
collects the dog's
bark.

And)

And George
is not *gorgeous, which is*
why I'm holding his
hand.

Carousel)

Carousel!
Happened on. But
no one to
tell.

Hours)

Hours,
gone—come! I have spent my life
trying to reattach cut
flowers.

Wisteria)

Wisteria
bedpost: a blossom for every time
we kissed,
Maria.

Leave)

Leave
wrecks be; the heart will
restore them. Leave
Rex be.

Wilder)

Wilder,
Rex. Mature poet (tweak
of nature). Man-
child.

Bear)

Bear
cub, vestige of my happy
self. Pardon if
I stare.

Blog)

Blog
entry: Every day, the poet walks
a different invisible
dog.

Clueless)

Clueless
thoughts begin to flower, lining up
along my brain's
avenue.

Lake)

Lake-man,
I temper, reflect, and amplify;
I pretend I'm
awake.

Drops)

Drops
of rain lay out their yoga
mats—and my pain
stops.

Crêpe)

Crêpe paper
hats at the alley party take me back
to my vampire days
in Dieppe.

Discretionary)

Discretionary joy!
Deep brown dead grass does not dampen
the man's mowing
session.

Bruised)

Bruised
blue flames light spring: this
is how crocuses are
used.

Late)

Late
check-out: 3 hours for only $30.
A cheap, mini-cheat
of fate.

Sirens)

Sirens
approach like you walking toward me in my bed
of dreams and then move on
to the fire.

Analyzed)

Analyzed
to breaking by the waves,
I repair to the nearby
canal.

Dawn)

Dawn
camellias. Sweetness of an orange.
Maple leaves waving. Love
gone.

Sex)

Sex,
ours at least, is flipping cars and
climbing, unhurt, from
the wrecks.

Soul)

Soul-sweeten,
my companion plum, and rot
with me in this
bowl.

Found)

Found:
Home from the beach, an argument
we thought the surf had
drowned.

Were)

Were
you mine? Faded birds in
the bindweed
stir.

Last Call

I Love the Poetry of the Old

I love the poetry of the old,
Strand, Yeats, Meredith, Lowell,
Even Keats if you count
The hundred years he lived in twenty-five.

In a sense it is English made young
Again, the years few again;
The codgers, if they can last long
Enough, are writing for their lives.

The Elk City, Oklahoma, Temporary Lake

i.

Above what was yesterday a slight concavity
Of as yet untumbled weed and dried grass in red clay,
Studded with gopher holes and rattlesnake-colored

Burr, a shallow dish of neglected soil between K-Bob's
Barbecue and the Holiday Inn, the mark a meteor
Might have made had it changed its mind

An inch from the ground, in this almost indiscernible
Crater, last night's wet snow melted and formed a body
Of water as beautiful as any on earth.

ii.

As a woman will sometimes lift a man's hand softly to her breast
And ask that it rest
There, motionless, until whatever brought
Her to that moment is over, so the startled
Lake appealed for my attention.
And it was not, in fact, until I leaned over and saw myself
Broken by the mirror the wind-skirmished
Surface made that there was anything in heaven
But heaven. No cloud to be clouded,
No bird to be misplaced by this impostor
Sky. And the sunlight, unable

To fathom the ankle-high pool, now darted, now deftly
Swung from point to point, feeding the hours-old colors.

iii.

Throughout the day
The lake drained,
Shrinking to the size
Of a deflated
Basketball, and, at the very last,
A lost contact lens.

iv.

Kneeling beside the late lake, I let a handful of what was now
Sludge run through my fingers, conscious less of great depths
Lost than of the modest surfaces unequipped to hold them.

v.

If you should come upon these stanzas
Like service islands on the interstate,
Those oases of false but quilted consolation

Most akin, especially at night,
To a printed poem, the way
They will shield the traveler

From the fear of, but only temporarily
The fact of, emptiness, pardon
My one-too-many commas, the pains taken

And the initial caps
Which, like armor, can be fitted
Over the weakest argument.

—As if they could be hindered,
Those elements that unmake love
Faster than we can make it,

The most careful of us spared.

Study for *The Ampersands of Time*

Shorthand for eternity. Abbreviation for lengthening
        days. In the dense air of too much, lightning

        followed by no thunder but raindrops audible
on leaves. The ampersand: stunt double

for the indispensable conjunction, a weird
        line doing backflips & yet all forward

        momentum. In a book of poems, the revelation
of its eagerness to lead, into temptation.

A matchmaker. No previous likeness necessary,
        the ampersand boasts, able to marry

        rancor & fried eels, for instance, without
breaking stride. A blackout, a whiteout,

        the fuzzy galaxy two astronomers
bump heads over, the heart between Venus & Mars.

for David St. John

A Neglected Botanical Garden

This must have been a slow year
for the patrons of the eucalyptus
and pine. Unopened camellias
wizen but cling to the dirty branches,
rocking just perceptibly, as a ship does
in a dead calm. The yellow bell lilies
ring true—freed from the bees' agenda
and dying, they tout their brownness,
they answer to no one. Come here
for the quiet, get the trees' free speech:
sentences begun, no endings in mind.
Eloquence is always by accident.
At the Hyatt next door, the lawn
is afraid of the earth, ashamed of its roots.
Pruning shears shape clone after clone:
in the name of beauty, roses
are maimed and a distinction drawn
between the fully- and the overgrown.

'There's no leaving you behind'

There's no leaving you behind
and for proof of that I thank
the glass roof beneath my nose.
Never empty: the sugary truth is
weakening my knees. Donuts
were never meant for the solitary
life; likewise dolphins, dice.
There's no leaving you behind,
sluiced the water to the river,
whispered touch to the shiver;
connection, conception, pow!
There's no leaving you behind
so let's not hear of loneliness
from here on in; come hither
as you wither: the grain of sand
should not be taken with a grain
of salt like an alt-metaphor
in a poetry textbook; Blake's
life matters, even now—
O clue-queen of the universe,
why does the sexy architect
storm the castle on our strand?
Every word is an "and"
if you're wearing the right hearing
aid. Once an earthling, always
an earthling, no matter which
nebula dusts you off, Mr. Lincoln.
There's no leaving you behind
is the idea the gum that's one

with Ocean Avenue is chewing on
and on as the long-gone speed
demon who lost the spearmint
flavor picks up the coordinates
on his sweetheart's rosebud lips.
Even seasons don't let seasons
go; they put their big fat arms
around the year like it's a warm
pole they're sliding down.
There's no leaving you behind;
not with heat-seeking feet
like yours. We're a remake
of a '60s movie. We say goodbye
but right away we're waving
each other back. The train
in this scene chugs away
one passenger short every time.
There's no leaving you behind—
not that I mind—you're so kind.
I remember the dinner (out,
ordering) we first surrendered
any pretense of compatibility.
There'd be no rhyme scheme
with us, no scheme at all to bind us
with the ribbon of inevitability.
We rely on redolence, mere
whiffs of this hope or that rope.
We don't love each other
per se, though we say we do
with bold, absentminded strokes
via technology and tongue,
as if we're oiling our jaws
with the words. It's more out

of loyalty to the fireplace
at eight o'clock (as we say
on the sailboat), and the bananas
in the bowl by the Warhol,
and the sea air outside the bay
window—the same sea
that won't let a single wave
go far, for long, before
reclaiming the broken mess
to the grace of its bosom.

ACKNOWLEDGMENTS

The loudest applause and deepest bow of gratitude go to LA's own Red Hen Press for printing *Waking Bodies* and *Boomerangs in the Living Room,* and for allowing Chatwin Books to reprint so many poems from those two books.

Many of the poems in this book were published (sometimes in variant form) in journals and publications including: *American Poetry Review, Antioch Review, Barrow Street, Beloit Poetry Journal, Black Warrior Review, The Book of Eros: Arts and Letters from Yellow Silk, Colorado Review, Cream City Review, Georgia Review, Greensboro Review, Harvard Review, L.A. Weekly, Los Angeles Review, The Nation, National Review, The New Republic, New York Magazine, Ploughshares, Poet Lore, Poetry, Poetry Daily, Poetry Ireland Review, Slope, Southern Review, Southwest Review, The Times Literary Supplement, Wide Awake: Poets of Los Angeles and Beyond, Yale Review, Yankee, Yellow Silk,* and related websites and anthologies.

Finally, I have three luminaries to thank not only for recognizing the poet in the man, as they edited and published the three volumes that form the backbone for this one, but more importantly for their friendship: the talented, indefatigable Kate Gale and tasteful, indestructible Mark Cull at Red Hen Press, and Phil Bevis, whose Arundel Press brought the comely *Beauty and the Books* into the world.

Index of Poems

REX WILDER

CPSIA information can be obtained
at www.ICGtesting.com
Printed in the USA
BVHW07s1639040918
526486BV00002B/139/P